Hands on Numeracy A   1

Margaret Share

Acknowledgements

I would like to thank my husband David and daughters Suzanne, Samantha and Emma for all their help and support. I would also like to thank Maureen Allsopp for her help and support. Thanks also to the children of Samuel Barlow, for their enthusiasm and inspiration.

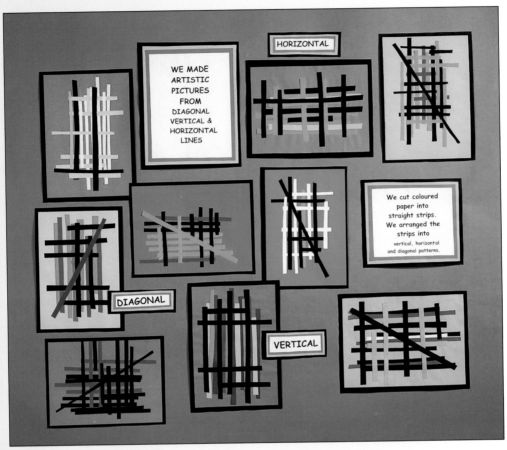

Horizontal, vertical and diagonal line art (page 47)

Published by Collins, An imprint of HarperCollins*Publishers*
77 – 85 Fulham Palace Road, Hammersmith, London, W6 8JB

Browse the complete Collins catalogue at
www.collinseducation.com

© HarperCollins*Publishers* Limited 2011
Previously published in 2005 by Folens as 'Numeracy on Display'
First published in 2001 by Belair Publications

10 9 8 7 6 5 4 3 2 1

ISBN-13 978-0-00-743934-8

Margaret Share asserts her moral rights to be identified as the author of this work

British Library Cataloguing in Publication Data
A Catalogue record for this publication is available from the British Library

Every effort has been made to trace copyright holders and to obtain their permission for the use of copyright material. The authors and publishers will gladly receive any information enabling them to rectify any error or omission in subsequent editions.

Commissioning Editor: Karen McCaffrey
Cover design: Mount Deluxe
Photography: Kelvin Freeman
Line drawings by Sara Silcock (Linda Rogers Associates)

Editors: Elizabeth Miles and Jennifer Steele
Page layout: Suzanne Ward

Printed and bound by Printing Express Limited, Hong Kong

Mixed Sources
Product group from well-managed forests and other controlled sources
www.fsc.org Cert no. SW-COC-001806
© 1996 Forest Stewardship Council
FSC

Contents

Introduction

Mathematics has been seen for too long as a subject apart, understood only by 'clever people'. Mathematics can be a colourful, exciting, interactive and interesting subject through which children can achieve success if their learning needs are positively met. Through a variety of aural, visual and practical activities all children have an opportunity to learn in the style to which they are most receptive.

This book endeavours to provide interesting and worthwhile mathematics activities at a variety of levels suitable for children from 7–11 years. It also provides the busy teacher with instant ideas for lively and interactive mathematical displays. The displays are designed to be assembled quickly and easily and used as a stimulus and context for learning. Work generated by the children in mathematics lessons can be added to displays to celebrate and consolidate children's achievements and understanding. Some displays can be used again and again in many different ways.

Each of the 33 themes offered provides suggestions for oral and mental work, ideas for practical and recorded activities and challenges in the form of the Activity Board to extend or consolidate children's knowledge.

Wherever possible, suggestions, instructions and diagrams are included for children to make quick and easy

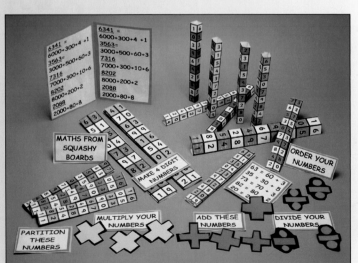

apparatus such as the intersecting paper plates used for fractions, time and angles work. Providing children with a plastic zip folder to store their own 100 squares, multiplication squares, arrow cards, digit cards, place lists, counters and little books can help to support growing independence. These materials can then be easily accessed for 'Show Me' activities in which the teacher asks the children a question and the children respond by 'showing' the answer.

Just as children learn in different ways, they need to record their work in different ways. Recordings can range from jottings on scraps of paper to 'Show Me' activities, diagrams or assembled apparatus. They may also take the form of little books in which a child can explain all he or she knows about a specific mathematical function, such as adding.

Generally, children find it difficult to explain how they have worked out a mathematical problem, and this is often due to a limited mathematical vocabulary. Making books can provide an excellent opportunity to practise the skill of explaining their work. The books can be varied in shape, for example concertina books can be shaped as cats or ice creams. Sliding books and fan-shaped books can be used to emphasise the order in which work needs to be completed, for example in recording the different strategies used to solve a problem.

The computer is a powerful tool for both generating mathematics and enhancing children's work. It is, however, important to make sure that it is used only when it is the best means of producing results. For example, the Data-Handling Crisp Investigation was enriched due to the variety of graphs produced using a data-handling package. Instead of spending time drawing graphs, the children had the opportunity to discuss and interpret their work.

Making use of the Internet and clip art to search for appropriate images allows children to take a more active part in producing displays. For example, the tickets, torches and signs used in the cinema displays enhance the visual quality of the work and make the activity more authentic for the children. Word-processing work for display not only gives a professional finish to their work but also lifts children's self-esteem when they see their final presentation. This is particularly useful for children who produce untidy but mathematically correct work.

I hope this book provides you with the inspiration to deliver and display exciting mathematics, leaving the children begging for more!

Margaret Share

Trains and Caterpillars

Display

- Create a Place Value display train as a starting point for work on whole numbers up to 1000. Make three rows containing nine train carriages. Add further rows if you wish to work with larger numbers, for example 1000–9000.

- Make removable place value cards attached to lollipop sticks, for example 1–9, 10–90, 100–900. (This display can be used for larger numbers, negative numbers and decimals.)

- Create a caterpillar display as a starting point for work on decimals.

- Use different coloured envelopes for the caterpillars' bodies and make rows of segments.

- Create removable decimal cards, on lollipop sticks for example, showing 0.1–0.9, 0.01–0.09, 0.001–0.009 and 0.0001–0.0009.

Oral and Mental Activities

- Use the displays to illustrate how numbers are made up, for example 258 is 200 + 50 + 8; 0.0125 is 0.01 + 0.002 + 0.0005.

- Point to numbers on the displays and ask the children to say them and write them in numbers/words, or ask children to show them using their own place value cards. Remove the numbers for checking.

- Choose a number and ask the children to show a number that is 1, 10, 100, 0.1, 0.01 or 0.001 more than the number shown.

- Withdraw numbers from the display and ask the children to explain their correct position and then put them back.

- Use the display to show that when a number is multiplied by 10 the digits move one place to the left. Ask the children to multiply a number on the place value chart by 1, 10 or 100.

- Use the display to show that when a number is divided by 10 the digits move one place to the right. Ask the children to divide a number on the place value chart by 1, 10 or 100.

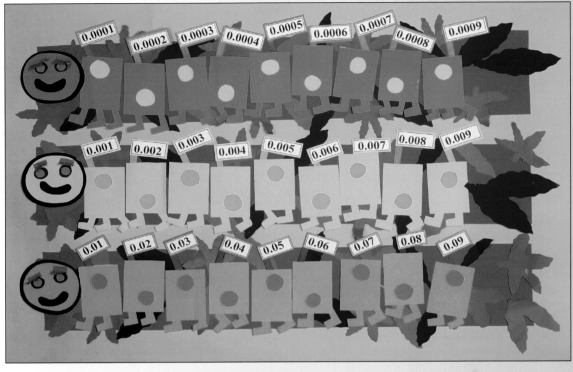

- Use one, two or three dice to generate numbers up to 666 and partition them, for example 3, 5, 2 = 352, 300 + 50 + 2.

- Use squashy boards (see photograph on page 4) to generate two-digit numbers, and use two boards together to generate numbers up to 1000, or larger by adding more boards. Read the numbers and identify the place value of each digit.

- Use squashy boards to generate decimal numbers by putting a point in-between the boards, for example 23.35. Read the numbers and identify the place value of each digit.

Practical and Recorded Activities

- Provide each child with a partially empty place value chart and ask them to fill in the gaps. Differentiate the activity by providing more or fewer numbers. Keep the completed chart as a learning aid to support work on place value.

- Work in small groups. Fill a small bag with multilink cubes, using only three colours. Red is 1, green is 10, blue is 100. Children select three cubes, say the number represented by the cubes and then record it. Extend to four multilink cubes.

- The children work in pairs. One child rolls a die to generate a number and decides if their number will be worth units, tens or hundreds. The game continues until each child has had six rolls of the die. The child with the largest/smallest or nearest to a given number wins.

- Use the place value charts to play Place Value Bingo. Make cards with numbers, for example 321. Call out ten numbers, the children cover their numbers using counters, for example 300 and 20 and 1. Check to see if they are correct.

Place Value Chart

1	2	3	4	5	6	7	8	9
10	20	30	40	50	60	70	80	90
100	200	300	400	500	600	700	800	900
1000	2000	3000	4000	5000	6000	7000	8000	9000
10 000	20 000	30 000	40 000	50 000	60 000	70 000	80 000	90 000

300 + 20 + 1 = 321

Place Value Chart

1				6				
							800	900
	3000							
				60 000				90 000

Activity Board

- Pin up a place value chart with only the numbers 1 and 90 000 shown. Ask the children to fill in selected numbers in the correct places. For example: Can you fill in 5? Can you fill in 800? Can you fill in 3000? 60 000? and so on. Use decimals, negative numbers and so on as an extension of this work.

Hands-On

- Create A Hand For Numbers display showing children's recording of number bonds. Display paper cut-outs of children's hands on balloons showing number bonds to 10, 20 and/or 100. Label the balloons with the number bonds shown by the children's hands.

Oral and Mental Activities

- Play 'Throw Me'. In this game the teacher shows four digits (fingers); the children have to 'throw back' the number of digits that will make 10. Children 'throw back' their number on the command 'throw me'.

- Stress the importance of 5 as the halfway number or holding point. Numbers are only one or two more than 5 or one or two less than 10. This is an important concept in number bonds.

- Use coat hangers and ten pegs to show number bonds to 10, 100, 1000. Turn the coat hanger round to show that addition is commutative, for example 4 + 6 = 10, 6 + 4 = 10.

- Use a counting stick which is marked into ten sections, but not numbered. Reinforce work on number bonds by telling the children that one end of the counting stick is zero, the other 10. Point to a calibration on the counting stick and ask how many more will be needed to make 10 or 'if 4 is taken away how many will be left?' Reinforce the importance of 5 as a halfway number.

- Play 'Show Me' activities using digit cards. For example, hold up number 4 and the children show the number needed to make 10.

- Extend the 'Throw Me' game by asking what would happen if each digit/peg was worth 10, 100 or 1000.

- Emphasise the importance of 8 + 2 being similar to 80 + 20 and 800 + 200, and so on. Use multilink cubes to show addition and subtraction bonds to 10, 100, 1000.

Practical and Recorded Activities

- The children draw round their hands on coloured paper and cut them out. Decide on the number bond they wish to display (1–10, where each digit is worth 1; 1–20, where each digit is worth 2; 10–100, where each digit is worth 10), for example 6 + 4 =10. Show six fingers and fold back the remaining four to illustrate the number bond.

- Ask the children:
  - What is the number bond you are showing?
  - What else do you know about this number?

- Ask the children to write 20 random numbers from 0–10. Ask them to join up the numbers to make 10 in as many different ways as possible. The children can write in the appropriate number next to any numbers left over to make 10. Repeat for numbers 0–20, 10–100, or 100–1000.

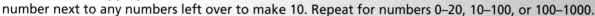

- Ask the children to show number bond rods using multilink cubes.

- Record on squared paper and use sticky dots to reinforce the concept. Add statements about the number bonds, for example 6 + 4 =10, 4 + 6 =10, 10 – 4 = 6, 10 – 6 = 4.

- Display a variety of coat hangers containing ten pegs. Write cards with number bonds 1–10, 10–100, 100–1000. The children can show the number bonds on the coat hangers and draw and label the number bond shown.

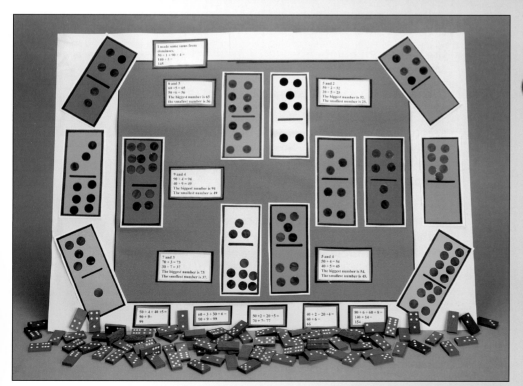

Activity Board

- Use dominoes to make number bonds up to 20. Record on domino shapes using sticky dots.

- Ask the children to write the addition and subtraction bonds for their domino. Extend by recording the addition and subtraction bonds to 100 or 1000 by making each dot on the domino worth 10 or 100.

Caterpillars and Dartboards

Display

- Create a Caterpillar display as a starting point and context for halving. Using split pins to join body segments, make two large caterpillars that have movable bodies. Display examples of halved numbers which demonstrate the rules of the game in which you add 1 to an odd number and halve an even number.

- Create a large dartboard in the shape of an apple for the centre of the display. Alongside, display small dartboards and caterpillars.

Oral and Mental Activities

- Display a selection of numbers below 20 for the children to halve and write the answers. Emphasise that halving is dividing by 2. Discuss how they halved the odd numbers (they probably added 1 and halved).

- Use cards with numbers up to 20 for the children to double as a 'Show Me' activity.

- Use cards with a variety of numbers containing some with a difference of 2, to double. Select children to answer.

- Create a set of number cards to halve or double. Select three children as part of a function machine. The first child feeds in the number, the second child says the function (halving/doubling) and the third child completes the operation.

- Give the children a short list of near doubles with a difference of 2, for example 25 and 27. Model how by taking 1 from the 27 you are left with 26. Adding that 1 onto the 25 makes 26. So, adding 25 and 27 is the same as doubling the number between them, that is 26.

- Display cards showing near doubles. Invite the children to double the numbers and explain their method of doubling. For example: 33 + 34 = 33 + 33 + 1 = 67.

- Provide a starting card with a number less than 10. Double the number and choose to add or subtract 1. Continue the game until the numbers become too big.

Practical and Recorded Activities

- Use a pack of cards numbered 1–40 and a 0–100 number line in graduations of 1. Ask the children to select a number from the pack, double it and add 1, then record their jumps on the number line.

- Draw the head of a caterpillar, write in a number less than 100. Add segments following the pattern:
  - if it is odd, add 1
  - if it is even, halve it.

- Continue until your caterpillar reaches 1.

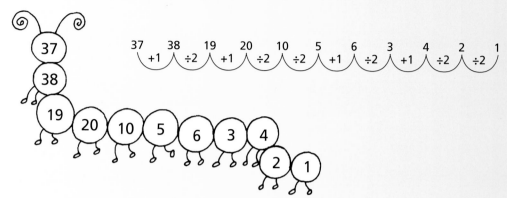

- Challenge the children to make the longest caterpillar from numbers under 100. Alternatively, use this game for doubling numbers:
  - if the chosen number is odd, add 1
  - if it is an even number, double it.

- Ask the children to identify the pattern.

- Give each child a blank dartboard and ask them to print the numbers 1–10 at random around the board. Double the numbers on the dartboard, continuing until the numbers get too difficult. Repeat for numbers up to 20. Mount the work and display.

- Demonstrate how to triple numbers, by doubling and then adding the original number.

Activity Board

- Display a large, empty 100 square. Place a pack of cards marked 1–49 next to it. Select a card. Working in pairs, one child points to the number space on the 100 square. The second child writes the doubled number in the correct place on the 100 square.

- Alternatively, small, blank photocopied number squares can be used. One child marks the number space to double on the 100 square. The other child writes the doubled number in the correct place.

Factor Search

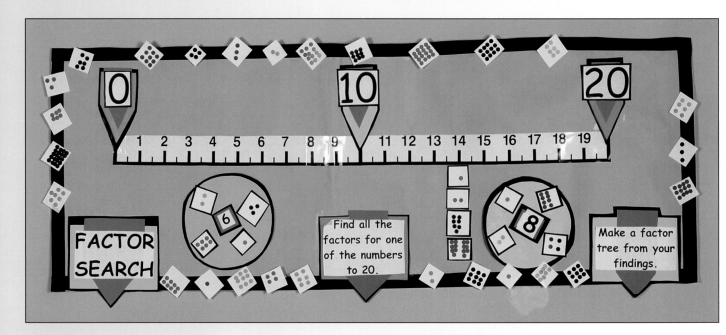

Display

- Design and create an interactive Factor Search display as a starting point for working on factors. Display a number line, labelled 0–20. Add yellow circles to display the factors of given numbers, for example the factors of 8 are 1, 2, 4 and 8. Make removable, laminated dice faces, each displaying factors of the numbers shown. Attach them around the display.

- Create a Factors display by displaying factor trees with branches containing the factors of a number on the tree. Around the trees arrange leaves which show factors of different numbers. Down each side of the display add square number grids demonstrating how square numbers have an odd number of factors.

Oral and Mental Activities

- Use an OHT and counters to show an array of 24.

- Model the factors of 24 using counters (one set of 24, 24 sets of 1, two sets of 12, 12 sets of 2, six sets of 4, four sets of 6, eight sets of 3, three sets of 8).

- Provide the children with 20 multilink cubes or counters and ask them to arrange them in as many ways as possible to show the factors of 20. (One set of 20, 20 sets of 1, two sets of 10, ten sets of 2, five sets of 4, four sets of 5.) The children record their work on squared paper.

An array of 24

$6 \times 4 = 24$

$4 \times 6 = 24$

- Ask the children to choose one number between 1 and 20, and investigate all its factors.

- Using the children's answers to the above questions, ask:
  - Did any numbers have only two factors? (2, 3, 5, 7 and so on, prime numbers.)
  - Did any numbers have an odd number of factors? (1, 4, 9, 16 and so on, square numbers.)

- Provide the children with sticky dots to investigate the factors of 15. They can record their work as annotated arrays.

- Ask the children what prior knowledge made finding factors of numbers easier? (Knowing their multiplication tables.) Which tables do they need to learn? The children should explain their answers in a sentence.

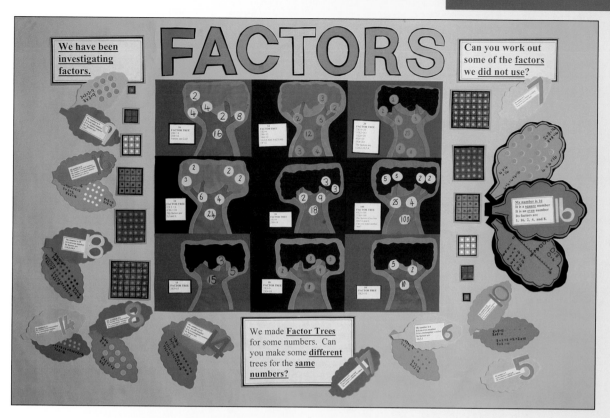

Practical and Recorded Activities

- The children choose a number which they want to make into a Factor Tree. Provide the children with multiplication squares to support their investigation. Differentiation will depend on the numbers that the children choose.

- Ask the children to answer the following questions about their factor tree:
  - Is your number odd or even?
  - Is it a prime number?
  - Is it a square number?
  - How many factors has it?

- Illustrate the factors on leaves that are displayed around their factor tree.

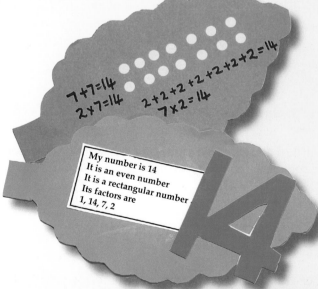

Factor Tree

Activity Board

- Use the number line in the Factor Search display to investigate which numbers are prime numbers (numbers that have only two factors). Which numbers are square numbers (numbers that have an odd number of factors)? The children can record a statement about their work, for example '16 is a square number because ...'.

It's Magic

Display

- Create a Magic Square display using work generated by the children. Add a large magic square with number cards labelled 1–9. Change the magic square numbers regularly.

Oral and Mental Activities

- Provide the children with digit cards 1–9. Using any method, ask the children to make 15. Record as a class the different methods found.

- Provide horizontal, vertical and diagonal grids of three squares containing a starter number between 1 and 9. Invite the children to complete the grids to total 15 using only the digits 1–9 and without using the same digit twice (see diagrams).

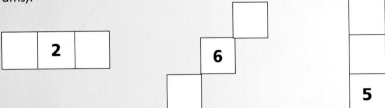

- Use a blank 3 x 3 square to demonstrate what is meant by a row, column and diagonal.

- Show the children an enlarged 3 x 3 grid with a magic number arrangement that always totals 15 and ask them what they notice about the grid (all the rows, columns and diagonals add up to 15).

Practical and Recorded Activities

- Provide the children with a 3 x 3 grid and ask them to write the numbers 1–9 on scrap paper. Use the numbers to investigate magic squares which total 15.

- Ask the children to investigate whether the magic square would remain magic if they added 10, subtracted 2 or multiplied each number by 3.

- More able children can move on to using a 4 x 4 grid (Note: odd-numbered grids are much easier to use than even-numbered grids.) Use calculators to support children when numbers become more difficult to calculate mentally.

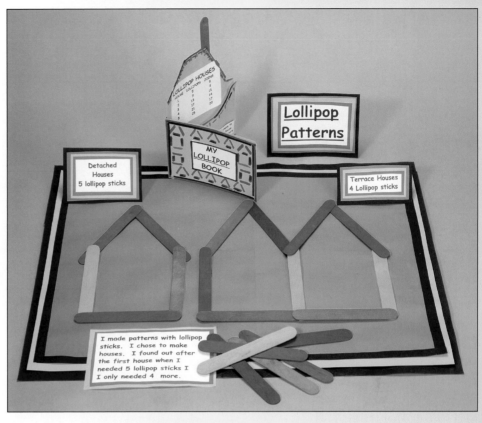

- Use coloured lollipop sticks and a baseboard to investigate number patterns through shapes. Find out how many lollipop sticks are needed to make a detached house. Repeat for a semi-detached house and investigate how many sticks are needed to add on one extra house, two houses and so on. What is the pattern?

- Use squares, triangles and other shapes to reinforce the concept. Can the children make any patterns of their own?

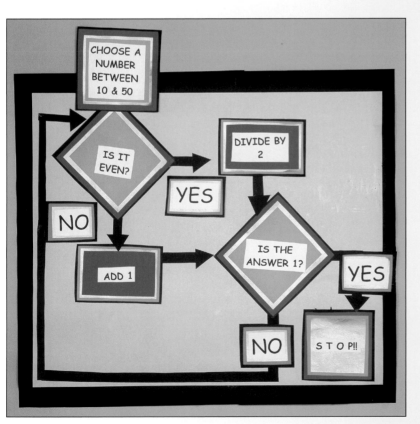

Activity Board

- Follow the diagram to create chains of numbers, for example:

25 + 1 = 26	26 ÷ 2 = 13
13 + 1 = 14	14 ÷ 2 = 7
7 + 1 = 8	8 ÷ 2 = 4
4 ÷ 2 = 2	2 ÷ 2 = 1

- Ask the children to find the pattern. (Add 1 to odd numbers and divide even numbers by 2.)

- Use numbers up to 100 to find the longest chain.

- Choose one pattern to display as a paper chain.

Funky Function Machines

Display

- Create a Function Machine display as a starting point and context for work on input–output machines.

- Make a set of cards which show the operations to be used (+, −, x and ÷) and a set of number cards that can be used to generate the mathematical problems. By changing the numbers and number of operations, this display can be used at a variety of levels using one- and two-digit numbers.

- Create a 3-D function machine from a small cardboard box. Leave a gap in the back to store the number and operation cards. Make a set of number cards (0–20) and a set of operation cards (+, −, x and ÷).

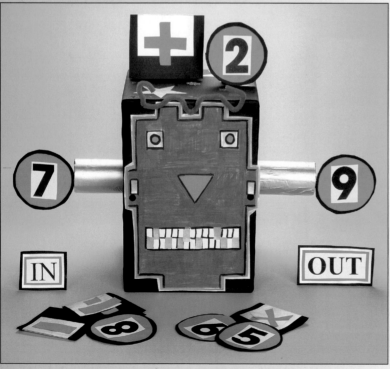

Oral and Mental Activities

- Work in groups of four children and provide them with a set of number cards 1–20 (or larger if the children are more capable) and operation cards (=, +, −, x and ÷).

- One child selects a number (for example 5), the second child selects an operation (for example x), the third child selects a number (for example 7), and the fourth child does the calculation (5 x 7 = 35). This activity gives children a very good opportunity to follow instructions carefully.

- Make the problem more difficult by working two function machines, for example 4 x 3 = 12, 12 ÷ 2 = 6. As the numbers become larger a calculator can be used to check results.

- Once the children understand how a function machine works, feed in a given number and feed out an answer so that the children have to work out the operation.

Practical and Recorded Activities

- In pairs, ask the children to work out the function when the answer is given with two operations (for example 21 and x 6 and + 3). Point out the importance of working backwards. Take away the 3 and then divide by 6. (The function was 3 x 6 + 3.)

- Ask the children to design their own 2-D and 3-D function machines and use them to input numbers and record the outputs. Differentiation will depend on the number size and on the functions used.

- The children can record their work in function booklets for display.

- Invite the children to challenge others to complete their function machine mathematics.

Activity Board

- Display a function machine. Ask the children to choose a number to enter and to record the output.

- Explore what happens when operations are swapped round.

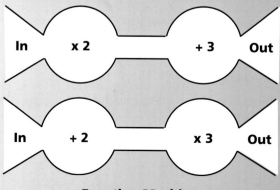

Function Machine

Up Your Street

Display

- Create a Street display. Use strips of display paper approximately 30cm wide and concertina into four sections. Cut out the shape of a house and windows, avoiding the folded edges. Open out to reveal four houses. Stick to black backing paper and add details. Number the houses with two or three digits as appropriate. Display as a street with envelopes showing the children's recorded work.

Oral and Mental Activities

- Show the children two digits and ask them which is the highest/lowest number they can make. Ask them to explain their answer. Order the two numbers made.

- Use place value cards to generate two-, three-, four- and five-digit numbers. Ask the children which is the highest/lowest number they can make.

- Read out two-, three-, four- and five-digit numbers for the children to write down in numbers and words as a 'Show Me' activity.

- Ask the children to show a number that is between a pair of numbers, for example: What is a number that comes between 257 and 278?

- Ask the children to find the number that is 1, 10 and 100 more or less than a particular number.

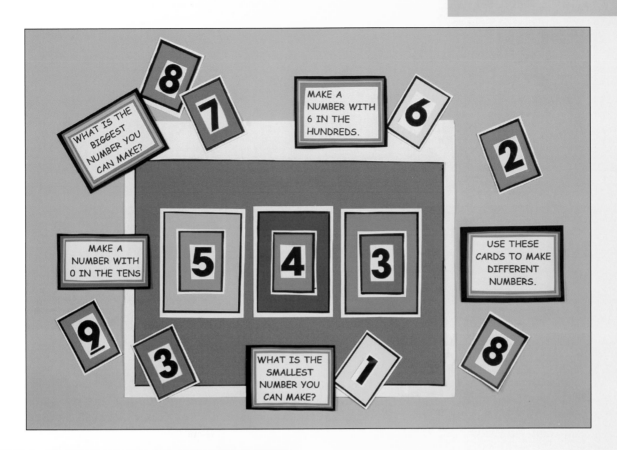

Practical and Recorded Activities

- Provide a baseboard and number cards 0–9. Randomly place three numbers on the baseboard. Ask the children to record the number and partition it, for example 543 (500 + 40 + 3). Investigate the highest/lowest number they can make using those three digits.

- Ask the children to make as many numbers as possible from the three digits using a digit only once in each number. More able children can work on four- and five-digit numbers.

- Ask the children to check that they have made all the possible numbers and to order their numbers from the smallest to the largest. Invite the children who have a system of recording to explain their system to the other children.

- Ask the children to display their ordered numbers by pegging them on a washing line or by holding the numbers and standing in a line. It is important that the order can be changed easily.

- Divide the children into groups and ask them to find all the possible numbers for a particular house on the street display.

- Ask the children to record on an envelope all the possible numbers they have found during the partitioning. Order the numbers, starting with the smallest or largest, on the roof. Ask the children to explain their system of recording.

Activity Board

- Invite the children to generate their own two-, three-, four-, five- and six-digit numbers. Challenge other children to find the number as quickly as possible by questioning. Before the challenge begins, generate questions that might be helpful, for example:
  - Is it more or less than 10, 100, 1000 …?
  - Is it an odd/even number?
  - Is it divisible by 10?

Flying High

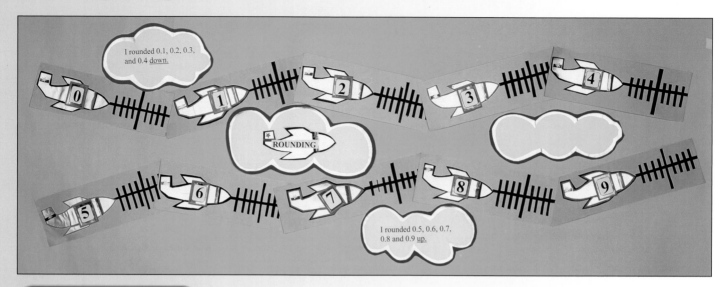

Display

- Create a Number Line display as a starting point for work on decimals and rounding. Make ten planes, numbering them 0–9. Mark the halfway point between each whole number. This display can be used and changed throughout the year to support work on negative numbers, fractions, whole numbers and decimals.

- Create a hot-air balloon as a starting point and context for work on rounding. Add the children's rounding-up calculations in the balloon and rounding-down calculations in the basket. Add clouds containing the instructions for rounding. The display can also be used for work on negative numbers, fractions and decimals.

Oral and Mental Activities

- Provide each child with a paperclip and a number line labelled 0–1 which has been divided into tenths but not numbered. Ask the children to put the paperclip on the halfway point.

- Show the number which is halfway between 0 and 1 on the plane number line. Ask what the number is called as a fraction and a decimal. Show the children how to write 0.5.

- Ask them how many tenths there are on their number line. How many tenths in 0.6, 0.5? Extend to 2.5, 3.4 and refer to the plane number line.

- Ask the children to point to different decimals on the plane number line, for example 4.5, 7.2, 5.9.

- Pre-record ten decimal numbers and ask the children to round them up or down. Record their work on a washing line numbered 0–10 by pegging their decimal number to the nearest whole number.

- Ask the children to record all the numbers which will round to 5.

- Ask them to use decimal fans to show a number which comes between 2.6 and 3.9 (see diagram).

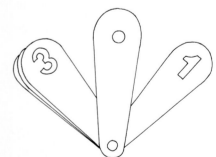

Decimal Fan

- Use a washing line labelled 3–4. Divide into tenths using pegs and ask the children to place decimals which round up to 4, or down to 3 on the correct peg on the washing line.

Counting Stick

- Use a counting stick (see diagram). Explain that one end is 0, the other is 1. Point to a graduation on the counting stick and ask the children to round up or down as appropriate.

- This activity can also be used for rounding to 100 and 1000, by changing the start/finish numbers on the ends of the counting stick.

- Ask the children to write the words 'up' and 'down' on a sheet of paper, tear the paper in two and use the words to answer questions. Say a number, for example 0.6, and ask the children to 'Show Me' if it should be rounding up or down. The children hold up the correct label (up).

- Use numbered 'flip-flaps' to generate two-, three- and four-digit numbers to round. (See instructions for flip-flaps on page 54.)

Practical and Recorded Activities

- Use a selection of dice, squashy boards (see page 4) and spinners to generate one-, two-, three-, four- and five-digit numbers. The children record the number they have generated and the two possible decade numbers it could be rounded to (24 would be 20 or 30). The children circle the correct number.

- Give the children a selection of numbers to round in this way. Display on the hot-air balloon.

- Extend this activity by explaining the rule for rounding to 100 and 1000 (49 and below round down, 50 and above round up, 499 and below round down and 500 and above round up). Use the same activity to reinforce understanding.

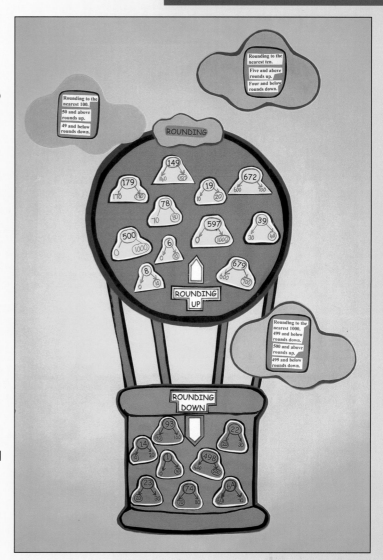

Activity Board

- Provide the children with a three-digit number ending in 0, for example 390. Ask them to write down four different numbers, only three of which will either round up or down to the number selected, for example 387, 392, 384, 394.

  Swap their recording with a partner who must find the number which does not round up or down to the start number (384).

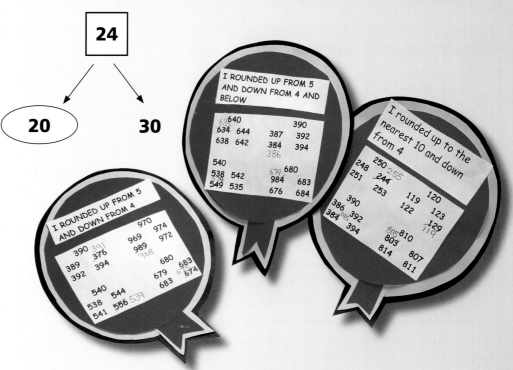

Pattern Detectives

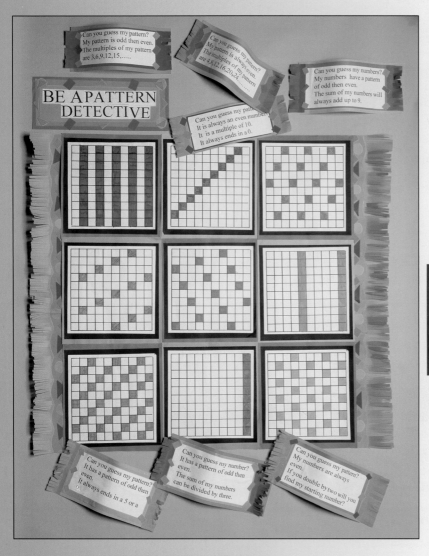

Oral and Mental Activities

- Use a counting stick to practise counting forwards and backwards in 2s, 5s and 10s.

- Use an OHT to show a multiplication square. Invite a named child to point to the 2x table. Ask: What do you notice about the 2x table? Expect answers like:

  - The numbers are always even.
  - The unit numbers repeat (for example 2, 4, 6, 8, 0, 2, 4, 6, 8, 0).

- Ask questions such as: What numbers are missing from this sequence 2, 4, ..., ..., ...,12, ...?

- Ask the children to hold numbers in their head, for example 2, 4, 9, 10. Which of those numbers are multiples of 2? Which are even/odd numbers?

- Explore different numbers for different attributes, for example the 5x table always ends in 5 or zero; the product of the 9x table always sum up to 9.

- Provide the children with multiplication squares with missing numbers to be completed or provide pieces of multiplication squares that need to be put back together.

Display

- Create a Pattern Detective display as a starting point and context for investigating patterns formed by adding or multiplying by 2, 3, 4, 5, 6, 7, 8, 9 and 10.

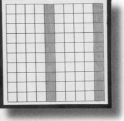

Multiplication Square

1	2	3	4	5	6	7	8	9	10
2	4	6	8	10	12	14	16	18	20
3	6	9	12	15	18	21	24	27	30
4	8	12	16	20	24	28	32	36	40
5	10	15	20	25	30	35	40	45	50
6	12	18	24	30	36	42	48	54	60
7	14	21	28	35	42	49	56	63	70
8	16	24	32	40	48	56	64	72	80
9	18	27	36	45	54	63	72	81	90
10	20	30	40	50	60	70	80	90	100

Practical and Recorded Activities

- Create a blank hundred square and cards showing the numbers 2–10. Select a number card and investigate the patterns made by placing counters or multilink cubes on the multiples of the number shown. For example, for number 3: 3, 6, 9, 12, 15 and so on would be shown. Colour in the recorded patterns.

- Ask the children to record the facts about the number pattern they have investigated. For example: the number is even; it can be divided by 2; it ends in 0, 2, 4, 6, 8; the pattern it makes is straight, vertical stripes.

- Provide the children with a triangular multiplication grid. Use the multiplication grid to find the six missing

numbers to open Tutankhamen's tomb. Begin by colouring the multiples of 2, 5 and 10. Then the children colour or shade any square number they can see. Finally, colour multiples of 3 and 4. What is left? There should be six unshaded squares (42, 48, 54, 56, 63, 72). The missing numbers are the most difficult multiplication facts for children to learn because they do not meet them in other tables.

Activity Board

- Provide the children with a 6 x 6 multiplication grid with some numbers blanked out to investigate. Cut another 6 x 6 multiplication square into three or more segments and ask the children to fit them back together again and place them on the grid.

Going to the Cinema

Display

- Design and create a Find Your Seat at the Cinema display as a starting point for work on number patterns in number squares up to 100. Add clip-art images of torches and tickets to enhance the display.

Oral and Mental Activities

- Show the children a large 100 square. Ask them what they notice about the numbers going across/down. What is the smallest/largest number on the number square?

- Count up and down in tens.

- Cover groups of numbers with blank grids and ask the children to guess the numbers underneath and explain how they worked out the missing numbers.

- Play 'Guess My Number'. A child chooses a number below 100, writes it on paper and gives it to the teacher. The class try to guess the number in three goes. Make sure the children know the questions that will eliminate the most numbers, for example: Is it odd/even? Is it above/below 50?

- Play 'Beat the Clock'. Provide the children with an empty 100 square. Challenge them to record the following numbers in the correct places in one minute: 10, 21, 31, 41, 99, 79, 59, 55, 56, 75, 85, 95, 44, 54, 64, 61, 62, 70, 80.

Practical and Recorded Activities

- Imagine going to the cinema but there is no one to show you to your seat and none or only some of the seats are numbered. Provide the children with a blank 100 square with none or some of the numbers shown and sections of a number square (tickets) that have been cut up into blocks of five. Their task is to find their block of five seats and stick the sections into the correct places. Ask the children to explain how they decided where their section went.

- Ask the children to total the numbers on their block of five seats. Calculators can be used to check calculations.

- Investigate which blocks of five seats add up to the smallest/largest amount and which add up to more/less than 50, 100 and 200.

- To extend this work ask the children to investigate which seat numbers would be next to theirs.

Activity Board

- Provide the children with a small 100 square and ask them to cross out blocks of five numbers or seats that join with a complete side.

- Investigate how many different totals they can make by creating their own blocks of five numbers.

3		
13	14	
Total 89	24	35

13	14	15
Total 102		25
		35

Adding Adder and Friendly Faces

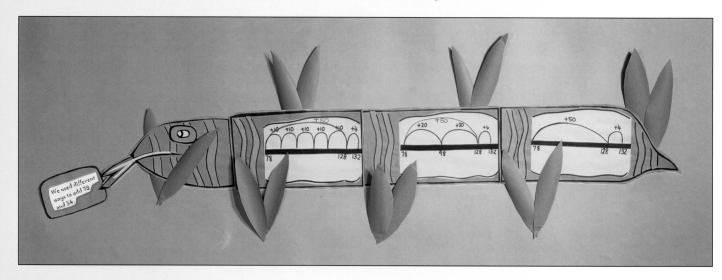

Display

- Create a display showing different calculation methods used by the children to answer given addition or subtraction questions. Find creative opportunities to display their methods, for example the Adding Adder or Friendly Faces display.

Oral and Mental Activities

- Use a counting stick to add on and subtract in tens. Give the children practice in rounding up or down to the nearest decade number.

- Use the OHT to demonstrate how to add 52 and 24 using an open number line – a line with no numbers (see diagram).

- Ask the children to estimate what the answer could be. For example, 52 rounds down to 50 and 24 rounds down to 20, so the estimated answer is 70 (50 + 20 = 70). Explain the calculation, stressing the importance of partitioning the numbers: (50 + 20) + (2 + 4) = (70 + 6) = 76.

- Ask the children to check the answer by turning the numbers around, for example 24 + 52, or by using a number line.

- Use the OHT to explain how to subtract 24 from 53 using an open number line (see diagram).

- Ask the children to begin by estimating the answer. For example, 50 – 20 gives an estimated answer of 30. Explain the calculation by partitioning the numbers as shown.

$$^{40}\cancel{50} + ^{13}\cancel{3}$$
$$- \ \underline{20 + 4}$$
$$\underline{20 + 9} = 29$$

- Ask the children to check the answer by adding the answer to the smallest number: 29 + 24; or by using the number line and finding the difference between 24 and 53.

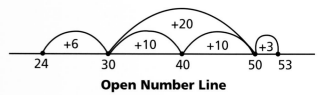

Counting Stick

Open Number Line

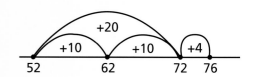

Open Number Line

Practical and Recorded Activities

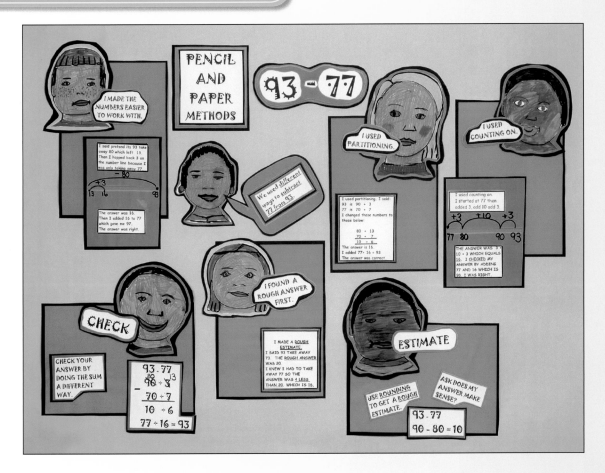

- Ask the children to calculate 78 + 54 in as many different ways as possible and display their calculations on a snake (the Adding Adder).

- Ask the children to calculate 93 – 77 in as many ways as possible and to write an explanation of how they did each calculation. Display the different methods alongside pictures of children's friendly faces.

Activity Board

- Ask the children to make their own books about either addition or subtraction (see diagrams).

- Ask them to write the vocabulary of addition or subtraction and explain what it means.

- Invite the children to select an addition or subtraction sum and explain how to do the calculation for another child to read.

- Display the work, and then ask the children to keep it and add to it as they become more competent.

- The books are an excellent way of seeing exactly what the children understand or do not understand in these areas.

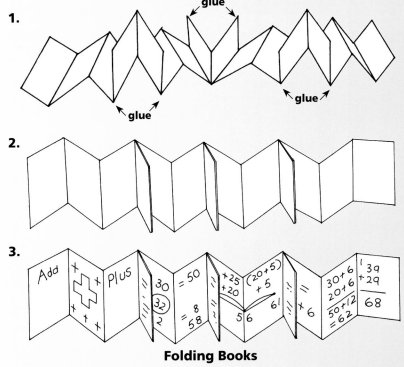

Folding Books

Toyshop Sale

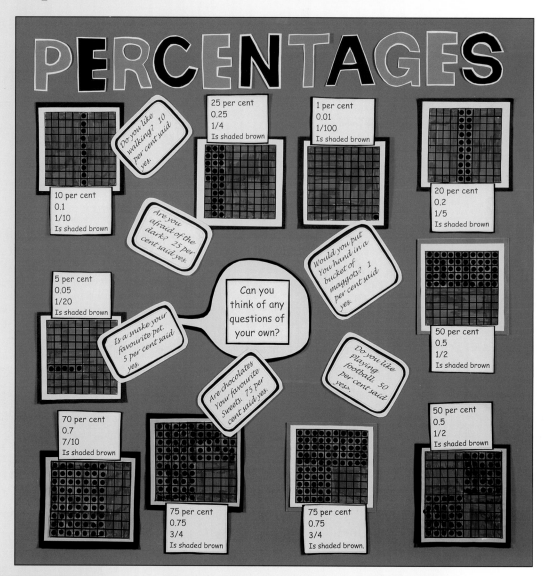

Display

- Create a Percentages display to present children's 100 squares, showing equivalent percentages, decimals and fractions. Add questions that children generated using their 100 squares.

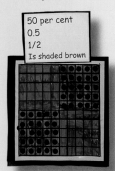

Oral and Mental Activities

- Display a large blank 100 square. Show the children the fraction made by putting ten counters in a straight line on the square. Ten counters shows 10 hundredths, one tenth, 0.1 or 10%.

- In pairs, using blank 100 squares, the children mark with counters percentages generated by the teacher (10%, 5% and so on).

- Prepare grids with different numbers of squares coloured, for example 50, 25 and 5. The children can work out the fractions and percentages they can see.

- Use a 100 square and a number line marked 0–100 to show the children the relationship between percentages, fractions and decimals on a number line. Draw the number line and label 0–100. Invite the children to show a half, quarter and tenth as fractions on the number line and add the equivalent percentages. Draw attention to the same fraction on the 100 square.

- Use a washing line and pegs. Invite the children to peg on equivalent percentages, decimals and fractions.

Practical and Recorded Activities

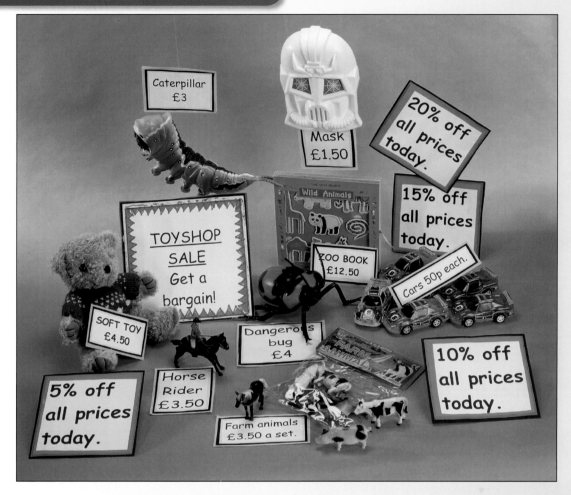

- Invite the children to choose a percentage and illustrate it by colouring it in on a 100 square. Ask the children to label the percentage they have chosen, and write its equivalent in fractions and decimals.

- Ask the children to make up a percentage word problem using their 100 square. For example: In interviews with 100 children, 10 said they were afraid of the dark. What percentage of the children were afraid of the dark? What percentage were not afraid of the dark? Mount and display the questions.

- Extend the children's learning by asking questions that do not involve 100. For example: There are 16 sweets in a packet of jelly drops. A quarter of the sweets are red. What percentage of the sweets are red?

- Display a variety of toys costing £10 or less. Tell the children there is a sale at the local toyshop. Display the percentage discounted each day and ask the children to work out the price of the displayed items.

Activity Board

- The children choose an object from the Percentage display and calculate its price with different percentage reductions (50%, 20%, 10% and 5%). Ensure the children understand that a 5% reduction can be made by halving a 10% reduction. Ask the children to make their own percentage books to record their calculations.

Sharing Sweets

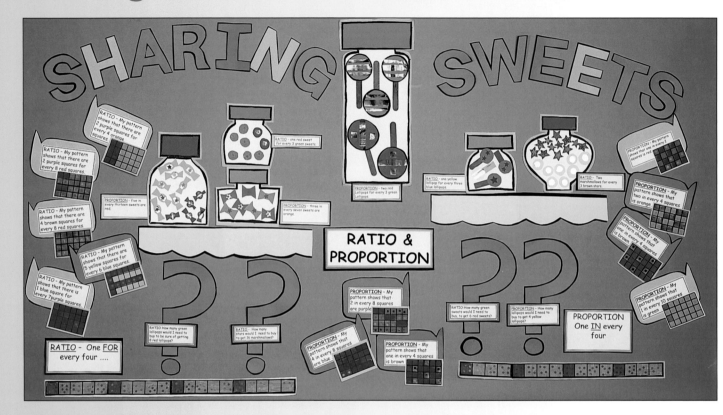

Display

- Create a Sharing Sweets display as a context and starting point for work on ratio and proportion. Make jars of sweets and lollipops showing different ratios and proportions within each jar. Add the children's statements about the ratio and proportion of the sweets in the jars. Add the vocabulary for proportion: 'one in every' and ratio: 'one for every' alongside pattern strips to illustrate each concept. Add the children's investigation work on ratio and proportion around the display, recorded on 4 x 6 grids.

Oral and Mental Activities

- Show the children four sweets: three red and one yellow. Explain that proportion involves comparing a part with the whole and is one in every whole number. Ask children to write a sentence about the sweets, for example: One in every four sweets is yellow.

- Show a variety of objects, such as farm animals, toys, multilink cubes and so on. Invite the children to make a statement about each group, for example: One in every four sheep is black. Display the objects with the children's statements.

- Show the children five sweets: four red and one blue. Explain that while proportion is comparing a part with a whole, ratio is comparing two separate parts and is one for every whole number. Ask the children to write a word sentence about the sweets, for example: There are four red sweets for every one blue.

- Provide a bag of sweets and two coloured bowls, one red and one blue. Share out the sweets, four in the red bowl, two in the blue bowl. Write statements to record the visual activity, for example: There are four sweets in the red bowl for every two sweets in the blue bowl. Invite the children to make their own ratios using the sweets.

Practical and Recorded Activities

- Ask the children to draw around their hand. Invite them to record statements to illustrate ratio and proportion about that hand, for example, ratio: there are four fingers for every one thumb; proportion: one in every five digits is a thumb. Record on a paper hand.

- Use pattern strips to help the children to develop the language of proportion and understanding of equivalent fractions. Provide each child with a pattern strip of 20 squares. Ask the children to colour in squares, for example: Colour one in every four squares red. Ask the children how many red squares there are in every 20 squares (five), so five-twentieths ($\frac{5}{20}$), or one-quarter ($\frac{1}{4}$), is coloured red.

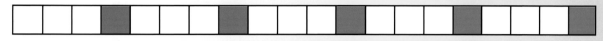

Pattern Strip

- Pose 'What if ....?' questions for investigation: What if the pattern strip was 40 squares long? (Colour 10 squares.) What fraction would be coloured?

Activity Board

Display the recipe for fruit salad and its related questions.

Fruit Salad

Serves four

Ingredients:

6 oranges
2 pineapples
4 pears
12 cherries
8 melon slices
¼ litre of juice

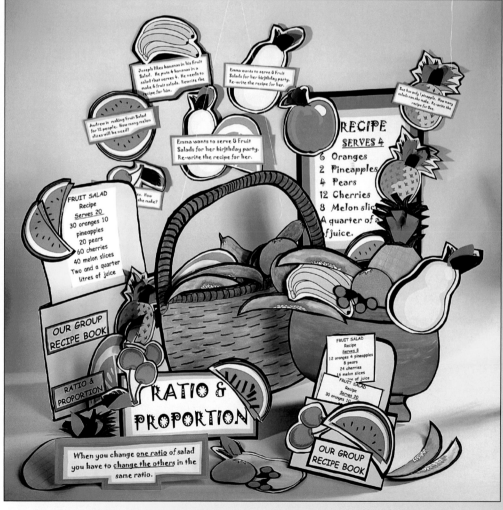

- Emma wants to serve eight fruit salads on her birthday. Ask the children to rewrite the recipe for her.

- John is making fruit salad for six people. How many cherries will he need? Rewrite the recipe for John.

- Sue has only four cherries. How many fruit salads can she make?

- Ask the children to make up their own recipe for fruit salad. Vary the number of people for whom they are making the fruit salad. Ask the children to put this information in their own Ratio and Proportion Recipe Book.

Below Zero

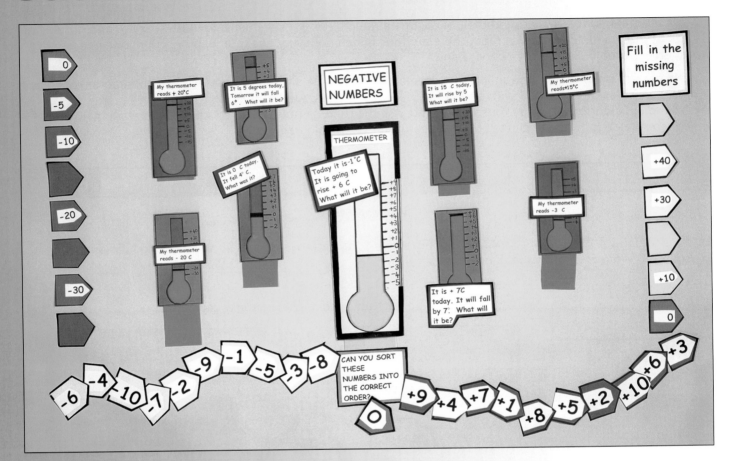

Display

- Design an interactive Below Zero display as a context and starting point for work on negative numbers. Display thermometers with a slider to show a changing mercury level which goes up and down, above and below zero.

- Display a number line showing numbers above and below zero for children to order. Add pentagon pattern chains, counting in fives and tens, with some numbers missing. This supports work in reading different graduated scales.

- Display the children's individual sliding thermometers alongside.

Oral and Mental Activities

- Use a negative number line to count on and back in ones, twos and fives.

- Show the children pentagon pattern chains with missing numbers. Ask the children to identify which number is being added or subtracted. The children must complete the chain, recording the missing numbers.

- Show the children a thermometer and explain how it works. Use a card demonstration thermometer to help them to read temperatures which are above and below zero (+ and –).

- Make cards with + and – temperatures, using numbers 1–10 or 1–20 depending on the scale. Invite a child to turn over a card and move the thermometer to show the appropriate temperature.

- Ask the children to look in their daily newspaper or use the Internet to find temperatures from around the world and to find the countries or capital cities with the hottest and coldest temperature recorded on a particular day. Record their information on a thermometer recording sheet.

Practical and Recorded Activities

- Provide the children with a number line marked –10 to + 10. Ask the children to make a timeline of their own life and to add information about what they could do at certain ages. Make comments about what happened ten years ago. A reply might be 'ten years ago was three years before I was born'.

- Record timelines on concertina and fan-books as they provide defined spaces which are useful for emphasising the order of events.

- Make small individual demonstration thermometers (see diagrams).
  - Fold the card into three equal sections.
  - Draw a thermometer shape on the middle third of the card and cut out (1).
  - Add the scale up the side of the thermometer.
  - Cut a length of contrasting coloured card to fit snugly into the folded thermometer and use as a slider to show the temperature (2).

1.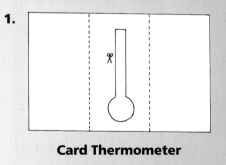

Card Thermometer

2.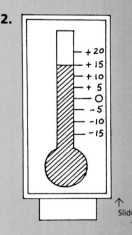

- Use a set of question cards starting at zero, so that the children can move the slider on their thermometers and show the temperature.

- Ask the children to write statements about the temperatures shown.

Activity Board

- Display a number of holiday brochures showing temperatures in different resorts around the world. Ask the children to choose a resort and record on a graph the hottest/coldest months throughout the year. In which month would they choose to visit?

Café

Display

- Create a Problem Solving Café display as a starting point and context for the children's work on problem solving. Make a variety of card ice creams, drinks, hamburgers and cakes, then add prices. Display a list of essential strategies for solving problems. Display the children's problem-solving strategies in the form of concertina food books. Include questions for children to solve.

Oral and Mental Activities

- Use the food items on display as a starting point for problem solving. Prepare questions for the children to solve.

- Model deconstructing a mathematics problem by writing the problem on a large sheet of white drawing paper. Cut the problem up into individual words. Fix the words onto a coloured base sheet with Blu-Tack. Read the question with the class and ask which words are not needed. Pretend to throw away the words that are not required, leaving only the words and maths that are needed to answer the question. Model two or three questions like this before asking the children to underline or, with a computer, cut and paste the important words and numbers needed in solving problems.

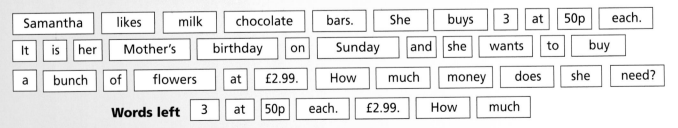

- Ask the children to help generate a list of strategies that they could use to answer word problems. For example:
  - Read the question twice.
  - Underline, deconstruct or copy and paste the important information.
  - Write down the mathematical operations needed to answer the problem.
  - Consider what you know already that will help you to answer the question.

Practical and Recorded Activities

- Make problem-solving books in the form of 'sliding books' to illustrate essential strategies.
  - Make a slider from a long strip of card divided into four and describe a strategy in each section (1).
  - Cut two parallel slits in a square of card to make a viewing window (2).
  - Thread the slider through the slits of the viewing window to highlight each strategy (3).

- Sliding books emphasise the importance of having a system for problem solving.

- Using the food items on display, more able children can generate their own word problems. Encourage the children to word-process the question, copy and paste the important words and then solve the problem.

1.

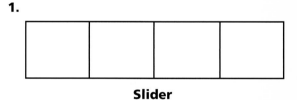

Slider

2.

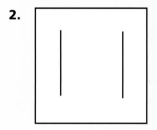

Viewing Window

3.

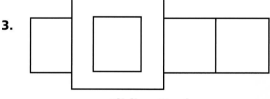

Sliding Book

- Design and create concertina food books to display problem-solving strategies and/or problems that have been answered or created by the children. As concertina books fold downwards there are defined areas between the folds on which to write. This helps to create a structure for the children's mathematics.

Activity Board

- Extend the children's learning by asking two- or three-part questions. For example: John buys a hamburger at 49p, a chocolate cake at 50p, an ice cream at 99p and a packet of crisps at 35p. How much does he spend? He wants to have his birthday party at the café. How much would it cost to take five friends and give them the same items? He discovers that one friend doesn't like hamburgers or crisps. What would be the total cost of taking his friends?

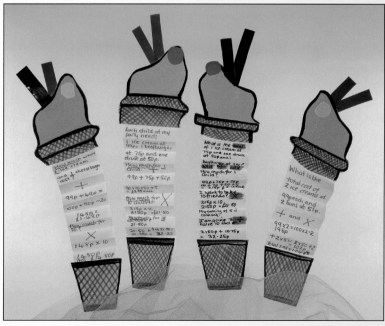

Favourite Food Fractions

FAVOURITE FOOD FRACTIONS

Display

- Create a Favourite Food Fractions display to illustrate the children's work on their favourite fractions. Paint and decorate plates or circles of cardboard as jam tarts and fruit pies. Display the pies and tarts showing different fractions.

Oral and Mental Activities

- Demonstrate fractions using intersecting paper-plate models. Invite the children to record the fractions they see.

- Encourage the children to develop an image of a specific fraction by visualisation. Ask them to close their eyes and visualise a fraction, for example a half. They can show the fraction on their own paper-plate models, repeat for quarters, thirds, and so on.

- Ask the children working in small groups to think of a fraction and show it on their paper-plate model. They could put their fractions into size order.

- Use paper-plate models for 'Show Me' exercises, for example: Show me two-thirds of your cake. How much is left?

- Use paper-plate models to play the game 'Make One'. Show a card labelled with a fraction. Ask the children to show the fraction that is needed to make one, using their plate.

- Draw a single horizontal line across the board. Mark the line 0–1. Invite the children to show halves, quarters, thirds, eighths and tenths on the fraction line.

Practical and Recorded Activities

- Make a model of a circular cake, pie or jam tart by painting two paper plates or card circles. Cut each plate down the radius as shown (diagram 1) and intersect the two plates so that one moves over the top of the other (2).

1. Cut each paper plate down the radius.

2. Intersect the two plates so that one moves over the top of the other.

- Use individual paper plates to show the particular fraction investigated. Ask the children the following questions:
  - What is your favourite fraction?
  - Can you label one piece of your fraction?
  - What will be left when your fraction has been eaten?
  - If you cut your piece of pie into two equal parts, what would each fraction be called?
  - What would the fractions be called if you cut each slice into equal parts again?
  Draw attention to the equivalent fractions found.

- Make cardboard models of rectangular sponge cakes. Add decorations, such as icing, cherries and cream, using coloured sticky paper. Add rubber bands and use to estimate different fractions, such as half, quarter, third. Every day, change and label the fractions shown.

- Create an equivalent fraction cake and display with chosen fraction cards.

- Use a washing line to gain a visual model of equivalent fractions. Ask the children to place the fractions ($\frac{1}{4}$, $\frac{1}{2}$ and $\frac{3}{4}$) in order on the washing line. Peg the equivalent eighths underneath.

- Ask the children to draw a number line 0–1 and mark on all the fractions they have found.

Activity Board

- Invite the children to find as many different ways of making 1 as possible, using two fractions. Remind the children they can be creative and use number lines, washing lines, pencil and paper, multilink cubes or paper plates. To extend, use three different fractions to make 1.

Sweet Shapes

Display

- Create a Chocolate Box Sweet display. Add large 2-D chocolate shapes made by the children. Display the chocolates on gold serviettes around mathematical descriptions of their shapes as a key to finding the appropriate sweet.

- Create a tabletop display of 3-D chocolate shapes made by the children. Attach labels with questions for the children to investigate.

Oral and Mental Activities

- Show the children a variety of 2-D shapes to name.

- Use an OHT to show a portion of a shape, for the children to guess. Write the name of the shape being shown.

- Display a 2-D shape and ask the children collectively to write down all the properties of that shape.

- Invite the children to visualise a shape described by you, for example: I have four straight sides. My sides are equal. I have four right-angled corners. I am a special quadrilateral. What am I?

- Hide a shape in a bag and ask the children to feel it, describe its properties, guess its name and record their answers. Pull out the shape and check.

- Play 'Imaginings' with 3-D shapes. Ask the children to imagine they have a box of chocolates in front of them. Paint the front, top and bottom of the box red and the back of the box blue. Paint the two other faces gold. Ask questions:
    - How many edges are there where a blue face meets a gold face?
    - How many edges are there where a red face meets a red face?

- Use 'Imaginings' to describe other shapes such as squares, rectangles, cubes and triangular prisms.

Practical and Recorded Activities

- Look at a box of chocolates. Invite the children to examine the key to the chocolates. Plan to make a gigantic box of cardboard chocolates and suggest the need for a key to locate their chocolate.

- Invite the children to choose a large 2-D shape and draw around it. Cut out the shape and paint as if it were a chocolate.

- Ask the children questions to help them to describe their shape mathematically. For example:
  - How many sides has your shape?
  - Is your shape a polygon, quadrilateral ...?
  - Is your shape a regular shape?
  - How many right angles has your shape?
  - How many corners has your shape?
  - Has your shape any curves?
  - What is the name of your shape?

- Ask the children to name their shape and record its properties.

- Provide the children with a selection of junk boxes. Deconstruct the boxes to examine the nets. Use the information gathered to construct their own 3-D chocolates in the shapes of cubes, cuboids, cylinders and triangular prisms. Paint and decorate them. Add labels with questions for the children to investigate.

- Make individual Shape Books investigating a chosen shape.

1. Fold and cut

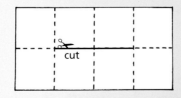

2. Open out

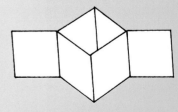

Shape Book

Activity Board

- The children can be challenged to name a shape after learning of its properties. Display a 'What Am I?' card and list the properties of a shape. For example:
  - I am a quadrilateral.
  - I have four straight sides.
  - My opposite sides are equal.
  - What am I?
  - I have four right angles.

Garden Symmetry

Display

- Design and create a Garden Symmetry display. Add butterflies to model reflective symmetry, bugs to model translational symmetry, and flowers with rotating heads to model rotational symmetry. Create a reflective symmetry title by cutting out two of each letter in the title. Place one set of letters to create the title 'Garden Symmetry' and another to create a reflection along a horizontal axis below.

Oral and Mental Activities

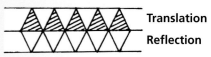

Reflective Symmetry

- Using an OHT, show the children examples of reflective symmetry (see diagram).

- Provide children with a rectangular sheet of paper. Ask them to fold the paper in half and produce pictures with matching halves by tearing and using ink or paint blobs.

- Provide each child with a large upper-case letter. Use mirrors to investigate their letter and see if it has an axis of symmetry. Ask the children to explain their findings.

- Show the children examples of rotational symmetry by providing them with squares and circles of paper. Ask the children to fold squares into four and circles into six. Cut small snips out of the folded paper. Open up and use the shape to demonstrate rotational symmetry.

- Invite the children to draw and cut out shapes from squared paper (see diagram). Rotate the shape around a central point to see if the pattern shows rotational symmetry.

  Rotate the shape round a central point.

- Use reflection and translation to make strip patterns. Provide each child with a cut-out triangle to produce a strip pattern by either sliding or translating the triangle or by flipping/reflecting the triangle (see diagram).

  Translation

  Reflection

40

Practical and Recorded Activities

- Make reflective symmetrical cut-out patterns on a butterfly shape. Cover the cut-out patterns with tissue paper.

- Make bugs, and slide them to make a translational pattern.

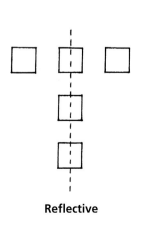

- Make a rotating flower by painting each quarter of a paper plate a different colour. Make a paper windmill as shown and number the sails 1–4. Attach the windmill and plate with a long mapping pin to an art straw and use the windmill to demonstrate rotational symmetry. (The paper plate is a teaching aid which allows the children to see clearly the 90° rotation of the windmill sail.)

1. On a large square of coloured paper, cut from each corner almost to the centre.

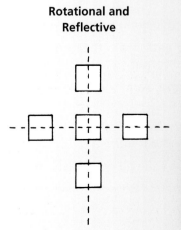

2. Fold over each wing and join at the centre.

Activity Board

- Use six squares of paper to show how many different patterns you can make showing reflective and/or rotational symmetry (see examples). Record the patterns on a squared grid. Display one of the patterns on the activity board.

Rotational and Reflective

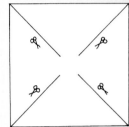

Reflective

Tessellating Bears

Display

- Create Tessellation displays from work generated by the children. Make tessellating chicks, dogs, bears and birds. Add paper clouds and a sun or real teddy bears to support displays.

Oral and Mental Activities

- Explain that to tessellate, a shape must fit exactly without leaving gaps or overlapping.

- Ask the children where they have seen tessellating/tiling patterns in their home. Show a variety of tiling patterns taken from sources such as magazines and the Internet.

- Using an OHT show a circle, square, rectangle and hexagon. As a 'Show Me' activity, ask the children to decide if the shape tessellates.

- Demonstrate that in order for a shape to tessellate it must be 360° at its junction. Use a regular hexagon to demonstrate this (see diagram).

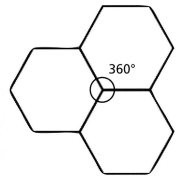

- Ask groups of children to sort flat shapes into those what will/will not tessellate. Record their findings on a Carroll diagram as shapes and words.

Practical and Recorded Activities

- Provide each child with a hexagon template. Ask them to draw around their template to make a tessellating hexagon pattern and colour it in.

- Use parts of the hexagon to make an animal of their choice.

- Decorate their tessellating patterns with coloured paper, shiny paper and glitter. Add ears, whiskers and beaks where appropriate to make dogs and chicks.

- Ask the children to draw around a hexagon, cut the hexagon in half and slide across (see right). Create teddy bears from this tessellation.

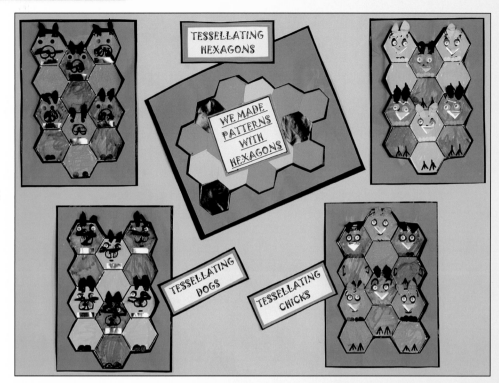

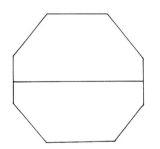 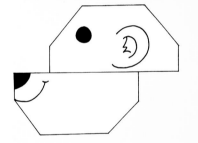

Activity Board

- Show the children how to make a tessellating tile by selecting a shape that will tessellate and cutting pieces out of it. Stick the cut pieces on the outside edges of the tile to make a new shape. Use the shape to make a tessellating pattern in the style of the artist Escher, for example tessellating birds. Decorate with wings and beaks and display in a sky scene with sunshine and clouds.

Frame It!

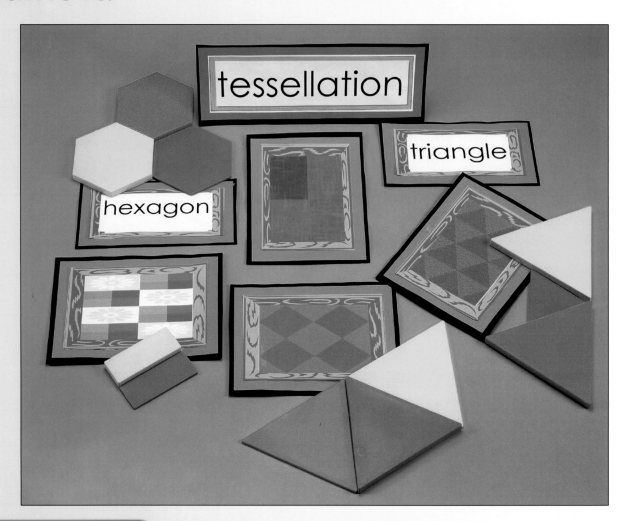

Display

- Create displays of tessellating patterns created by the children using shape tools in a DTP package.

- Import images into picture frame borders using clip art or the Internet. Display as pictures in an art gallery, adding relevant 2-D shapes.

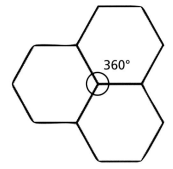

Oral and Mental Activities

- Show the children a variety of 2-D shapes and ask if they tessellate. Demonstrate that in order for a shape to tessellate regularly it must be 360° at its junction. Use a regular hexagon on an OHT to illustrate this concept.

- Using an OHT, investigate which shapes will and will not tessellate.

- Ask the children to visualise images from the environment that are made up of tessellating shapes, for example honeycombs, chicken wire and paving stones.

- Look at the work of famous artists, such as Escher and Kandinsky, for evidence of tessellation in their work.

- Provide the children with a variety of patterns and pictures to sort into groups of those that tessellate and those that do not (appropriate images can be found on the Internet). Ask the children to describe why they have made a particular choice.

Practical and Recorded Activities

- Give the children a box of shapes and in groups decide by investigation which shapes tessellate and which do not.

- Encourage the children to cut out and stick shapes to make tessellating patterns.

- Use clip art to create an easel as a baseboard for the children to create their own computer-generated tessellating patterns. Encourage the children to use the Internet to investigate famous artists such as Escher and Kandinsky who used tessellation in their art.

- Use the shape tool on a computer-draw program to create pictures which demonstrate tessellation. Choose colours and paint effects to create interesting detail.

- Ask the children to search clip art and the Internet for tessellating pattern images. Import the images into clip-art frames, print out and mount and display alongside 2-D shapes (see photograph on page 44).

Activity Board

- The Internet can be used to research and locate artists who use tessellation in their work. The children can use the Internet to locate examples of Islamic and Roman Art, print the examples and sort into those which tessellate and those which do not.

Royal Jewels

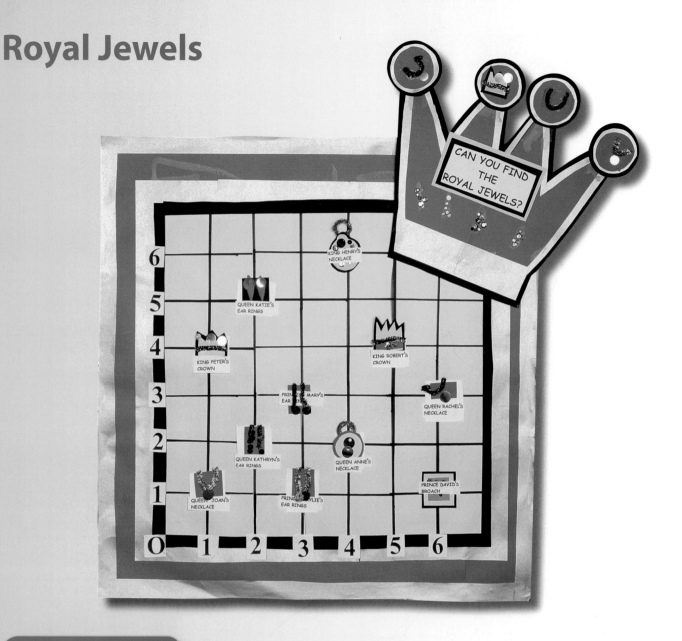

Display

- Design and create a Royal Jewels co-ordinates display. Ask the children to make exciting royal treasures to hide in the grid.

- Hide the title of the display in a co-ordinates grid for the children to work out.

Oral and Mental Activities

- Explain the terms: horizontal, vertical and axis and demonstrate how to find co-ordinates on a grid. Model the explanation on a 5 x 5 grid, labelled 1, 2, 3, 4, 5 on the horizontal axis and 1, 2, 3, 4, 5 on the vertical axis. Stress the importance of reading the horizontal axis first.

- Create a set of ten cards with positions relating to the 5 x 5 grid, such as 1, 5; 5, 3 and so on. The children select a card and place a counter on the grid. Ask the class which co-ordinates were written on the card.

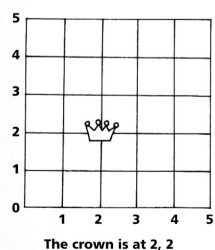

The crown is at 2, 2

Practical and Recorded Activities

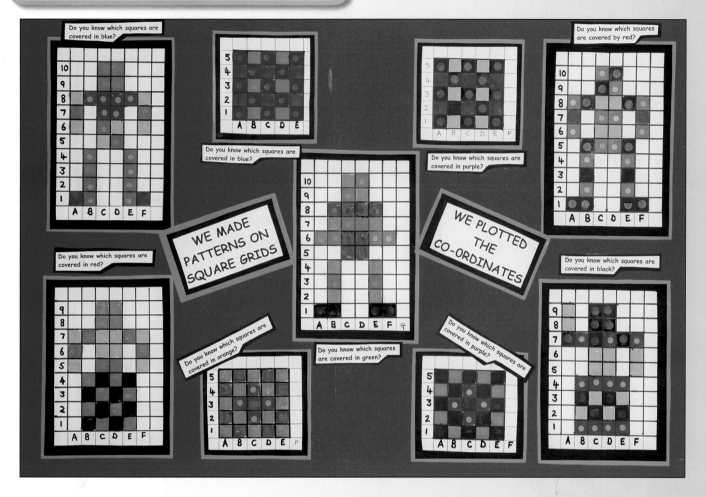

WE MADE PATTERNS ON SQUARE GRIDS

WE PLOTTED THE CO-ORDINATES

Do you know which squares are covered in blue?

Do you know which squares are covered by red?

Do you know which squares are covered in blue?

Do you know which squares are covered in purple?

Do you know which squares are covered in red?

Do you know which squares are covered in black?

Do you know which squares are covered in orange?

Do you know which squares are covered in green?

Do you know which squares are covered in purple?

- A fun way to support the children in understanding the terms horizontal, vertical and diagonal is to create line art, by cutting strips of coloured paper and arranging them horizontally, vertically and diagonally, and sticking them on to a coloured background (see photograph on page 2).

- Provide the children with grids to design a tiling pattern by colouring squares in different colours. Make a key to show the co-ordinates of different colours of the pattern, for example red can be found in squares B, 4; C, 2 and D, 1.

- Ask the children to design and make a treasure for the royal jewels co-ordinates grid. Write the co-ordinates for their treasure on the back of it, then place their treasure at its location.

Activity Board

- Ask the children to plot a regular shape on a 5 x 5 grid recording its co-ordinates.

- Challenge the children to plot the co-ordinates for a simple shape, for example a house. They record their co-ordinates and display for other children to plot.

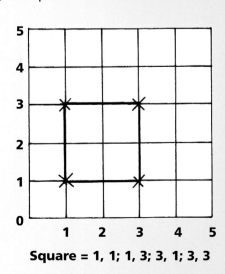

Square = 1, 1; 1, 3; 3, 1; 3, 3

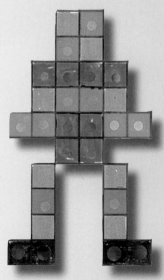

Angles in Space

Display

- Create an Angles in Space display as a starting point for work on angles. Design and make a large articulated robot, using split pins or mapping pins to attach the movable joints. Enlarge protractors and display for the children to use as a model for estimating angles. Display the children's angle measures and random space angles around the robot.

Oral and Mental Activities

- Provide the children with intersecting card circles in two colours (see diagram). Use card circles, not plates, because card gives a much more defined right angle.

- Ask the children to show quarter, half and three-quarter turns using the card circles; the different colours will show the angles very clearly.

- Ask the children to 'Show Me' a right angle, and angles that are more than or less than a right angle.

- Give the children a rectangular sheet of paper. Ask them to fold it in half, then half again (1), and to tear the centre piece (2), so they are left with a rough circle (3). Fold and use as an angle finder to find angles smaller or larger than a right angle (4).

1. **Cut each card circle down the radius.**

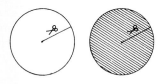

2. **Intersect the two circles so that one moves over the top of the other.**

1. **Fold.**   2. **Tear.**   3. **Rough circle.**   4. **Fold to form an angle finder.**

48

- Use homemade angle measures made out of card or wooden lollipop sticks to measure angles that are more or less than a right angle.

- Use the angle measures to demonstrate right angles, acute angles, obtuse angles and reflex angles.

- Select two children. One child will be the robot, one child the programmer. Child A, the robot, follows the instructions of Child B, the programmer. For example:
  – Left 90° – Forward 10 – right 90° – Turn 180° – Turn 360°

- Ask the children:
  - What happened when the child turned 180°?
  - What happened when the child turned 360°?

- Programme Pip, Pixie or Roamer to move through chosen angles.

- Use computer LOGO to support work on angles (see LOGO activities, page 50).

Practical and Recorded Activities

- Allow groups of children to move the display robot's joints to estimate and measure the angles.

- Use the intersecting card circles to explore different angles. Choose a favourite angle to label and display.

- Ask the children to create angles that are more or less than a right angle using the angle measures, and to label and display their work. Progress to measuring the angles with more accuracy using protractors.

- Ask the children to make random space angles using a ruler. Draw a line on a circle of silver paper and show acute, obtuse and right angles by rotating the ruler. Measure the angles accurately using a protractor. Stick coloured dots on the line to show the angle measured.

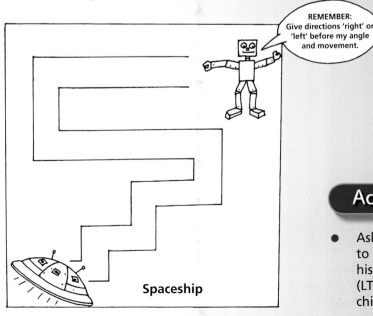

REMEMBER:
Give directions 'right' or 'left' before my angle and movement.

Spaceship

Random Space Angles

Activity Board

- Ask the children to give the robot LOGO commands to guide him back through the maze to the safety of his spaceship. For example: FORWARD (FD) 20 LEFT (LT) 90° and so on. Extend this activity by asking the children to design their own maze for the robot.

Plotting with LOGO

Display

- Create a display of children's work showing shape drawings using LOGO. Mount or import the work on a clip-art drawing of an open book.

Oral and Mental Activities

- It is important, when using LOGO or the Roamer to plot angles and distances, that the children see everything from the perspective of the turtle, imagining that they are in its nose. To emphasise this, make pop-on noses for the children to tie on their heads when following simple routes. Invite a child to be the turtle and ask them to follow simple commands. For example:
  - LT or LEFT followed by an angle in degrees.
  - RT or RIGHT followed by an angle in degrees.
  - FD or FORWARD followed by a number.

- Ask the children to plot their route from the door to their seat. They must count their paces and note each time they make a change of direction. Ask them to state if their turns are right angles or not.

- Place chairs or cardboard boxes randomly around a room. Choose two children: one gives instructions using LOGO language to a blindfolded child who then navigates round the chairs or boxes. Give each child a 'minder', to ensure they don't get hurt. Record the instructions, for example: RT 90°, FD 6. The children can then retrace their moves.

- Work in pairs with a screen between the pair. Invite one child to describe a drawn route or shape using LOGO instructions for the other child to draw on squared paper. Afterwards, compare the two drawings.

Practical and Recorded Activities

- Make a simple angle finder showing a turtle head and the turn of 90° LT and RT and 180° LT and RT, to support children when using computer LOGO.

- Use LOGO to draw a series of shapes. To make a square, use the commands REPEAT 4 (FD 40 RT 90). This command will instruct the screen turtle to repeat the instructions in the brackets four times. To use the screen turtle to make other polygons, use the formula REPEAT S (number of sides) (FD 40 RT 360 divided by the number of sides).

- Draw circles, triangles, hexagons and octagons using LOGO. Ask the children to explain how they investigated their shape, and word process the LOGO instructions for drawing the shape on an open book taken from clip art.

- Create a maze on cm² paper and import a TV screen border from clip art. Show a mouse as the starting point and a piece of cheese as the finishing point. The object of the activity is for the children to plot a route using LOGO language for the mouse to get the cheese. Extend by finding the shortest/longest route and design a more complicated maze.

Activity Board

- Invite the children to design their own games, for example writing instructions to find the Mary Rose or Tutankhamen's tomb. Include exciting features such as treasure rooms and dangerous places. Dangerous features could be 'jumped over' using PENUP and PENDOWN. Ask the children to record their routes and then pass them to another child to follow.

Fencing Fields

Display

- Create a 3-D fencing in the Farm Animals display as a starting point and context for work on perimeter. Present a variety of problems for the children to solve.

Oral and Mental Activities

- Provide each child with a 2-D shape. Invite them to run their finger around the outside of the shape. Tell them that the outside of the shape is called the perimeter. Stress that perimeter is a measurement of length or distance.

- Use a shoebox and a piece of ribbon or string to measure perimeter. Wrap the ribbon or string around the top of the box and cut to the exact length. Show the ribbon or string and measure it using a metre stick. Use this activity to emphasise that perimeter is a measure of length. Provide the children with a variety of small boxes to measure the tops in the same way.

- Use an OHT to show a variety of shapes on dotted grids. Select a child to run their finger around the shape projected on the wall or to draw on the acetate to show the perimeter of a given shape.

- Using geo-boards and elastic bands invite the children to make different shapes. Explain to the children that the elastic band is the perimeter. Ask them to transfer their shape onto dotted paper and label and measure the perimeter of each shape.

- Use an OHT to show square and rectangular shapes on cm² grids. Prepare strips of cm² paper showing the number of squares required to enclose the perimeter.

- Show the children a rectangle. Look carefully at the shape and ask if anyone can find an easy way to calculate the perimeter of a rectangle. Introduce the formula 2 x (length + breadth).

Practical and Recorded Activities

- Provide fields on square grids with different perimeters for the children to calculate. Investigate how much fencing is needed for each field containing different farm animals. Move animals into different fields to generate a variety of perimeter problems.

- Ask the children to bring a photograph from home and explain that they are going to make a cardboard photograph frame to fit it.

- Place a photograph on a cm² grid on an OHT and explain how we calculate the perimeter of the photograph (two lengths + two breadths).

- Ask the children to record the perimeter of their photograph using squared paper. This will then be their template for cutting the window in their photograph frame.

- Ask the children to cut out the window, attach their photograph and decorate their frames using brightly coloured sticky paper.

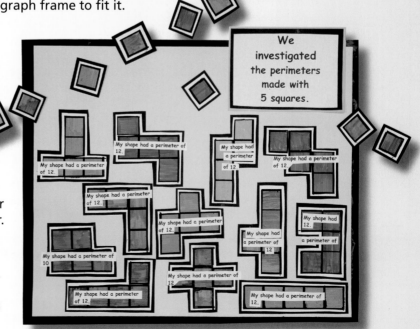

Activity Board

- Investigate how many different perimeters the children can make using five squares? Display and label the work.

Zoo Enclosures

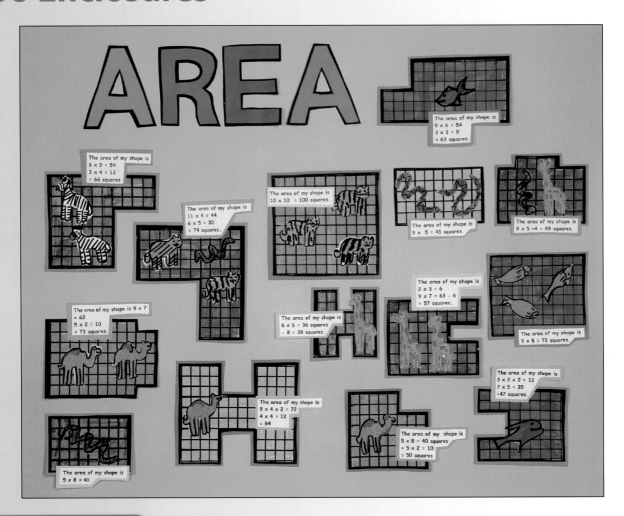

The area of my shape is
9 × 6 = 54
3 × 3 = 9
= 63 squares.

The area of my shape is
6 × 9 = 54
3 × 4 = 12
= 66 squares.

The area of my shape is
11 × 4 = 44
6 × 5 = 30
= 74 squares.

The area of my shape is
10 × 10 = 100 squares.

The area of my shape is
9 × 5 = 45 squares.

The area of my shape is
9 × 5 +4 = 49 squares.

The area of my shape is 9 × 7
= 63
5 × 2 = 10
= 73 squares.

The area of my shape is
6 × 6 = 36 squares
– 8 = 28 squares.

The area of my shape is
2 × 3 = 6
9 × 7 = 63 – 6
= 57 squares.

The area of my shape is
9 × 8 = 72 squares.

The area of my shape is
9 × 4 × 2 = 72
4 × 4 = 12
= 84

The area of my shape is
3 × 2 × 2 = 12
7 × 5 = 35
=47 squares.

The area of my shape is
5 × 8 = 40 squares
+ 5 × 2 = 10
= 50 squares

The area of my shape is
5 × 8 = 40

Display

- Create an Area display illustrating the children's plans of enclosures designed for different zoo animals.

Oral and Mental Activities

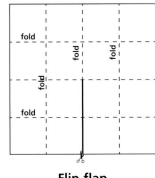

Flip-flap

- Provide each child with a 2-D shape. Invite them to run a finger over the surface of the shape. Tell them that the surface is called the area. Distinguish between perimeter and area.

- Use an OHT to show rectangular and squared shapes on squared paper. The children count the squares within the perimeter line. Use a 4 × 4 flip-flap (see right), and ask the children to record the areas of the folded shapes that you show them.

- Make your own flip-flaps using a square of paper. Fold the square in half, and half again, and repeat twice more. Open out the square to reveal a 4 × 4 grid with an area of 16 squares (see diagram).

- Ask the children to 'Show Me' a shape with, for example, an area of six squares, by flipping and folding their grid over. One cut to the middle of the half fold will allow greater flexibility of areas.

- Use geo-boards and elastic bands to find areas by counting squares. Investigate the different shapes that can be made using the same number of squares.

- Use an OHT to develop the idea of counting squares and bits of squares. Make large blots on squared acetate sheets for the children to estimate how many squares the blots cover.

Practical and Recorded Activities

- To understand that area is a measurement of surface, ask the children to draw straight horizontal, vertical and diagonal lines on paper using a pencil and ruler. Then ask them to colour in the patterns made by the lines. Emphasise how the whole surface or area of the paper is covered with individual colours. Ask the children to cut out any red areas of the picture, yellow areas and so on.

- Design a compound for an animal in the zoo. Work out the area of their enclosure, then colour and cut it out. Draw and cut out the animals to go inside.

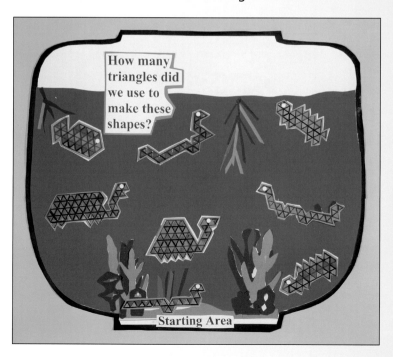

- Ask the children to draw their own sea creature using triangular paper. Count the number of triangles their sea creature covers. Ask the children to make a statement about their sea creature, for example: The sea snake covers 30 triangles.

- The children should learn and use the formula of length x breadth to calculate area and learn how to calculate bits that have been added on.

Activity Board

- Each lion in the zoo needs an area of 4cm². Provide a grid with an area of 30cm². How many lions could live in this compound? Vary the question daily. For example: An elephant needs 8cm². How many elephants could live in a compound that is 60cm²?

Red Riding Hood

Display

- Create a Red Riding Hood display as a starting point and context for work on estimating and measuring in metres and centimetres.

- Create the figure of a wolf, with different lengths of ribbon and a pocket watch hanging from the pocket for the children to measure. Make different-sized wolf ears, tails and teeth which can be changed to add variety to the display. Create Red Riding Hood and make a basket containing items such as bread and honey for Grandma, which can also be measured.

- Display the children's measuring work in paper baskets around Red Riding Hood and the wolf.

Oral and Mental Activities

- Show the children a metre stick. Ask them to demonstrate their interpretation of a metre by using their arms. Check some of their interpretations with the metre stick. Was their estimate short or long?

- Wrap a long length of ribbon around a hand. Slowly unwind the ribbon and ask the children to estimate how long it is. Ask three children to measure it. A child holds each end while the third measures. Ask if any children are changing their estimates as they see the ribbon being measured. Repeat this exercise two or three times with different lengths of ribbon.

- Provide the children with a standard-size sheet of rectangular paper.

  - Fold the paper into four strips lengthways (1). Cut the strips and ask the children to estimate if the strips will make a length longer or shorter than a metre (2).

  - Fix the paper strips together using adhesive tape and check the children's estimates against a metre stick. Adjust their metre measure to measure a metre (3).

1. **Fold the paper into four strips lengthways.**

2. **Cut the strips**

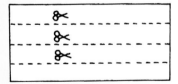

3. **Fix the paper strips together and adjust to measure 1 metre.**

4a. **Fold the measure into half and quarters.**

$\frac{1}{4}$	$\frac{1}{4}$	$\frac{1}{2}$	$\frac{1}{4}$	$\frac{1}{4}$

4b.

100 centimetres = 1 metre

- Ask the children to fold their measure in half and write $\frac{1}{2}$. Then fold the measure into quarters and write $\frac{1}{4}$ in each quarter (4a).
- Across the back of the measure, write '100 centimetres = 1 metre' (4b).

Practical and Recorded Activities

- Provide the wolf's ribbons in a variety of lengths for the children to estimate and measure. (More or less than a metre, half a metre, quarter of a metre, and so on.) Ask the children to find the difference between their estimate and measure. Record.
- Provide Red Riding Hood's basket full of items, such as ribbons, a cake and Grandma's bonnet, for the children to measure. The children can estimate and measure each item, and then record the difference between the estimation and the correct measurement.
- Make woven heart baskets, popular as Christmas decorations in Denmark, for the children to display their records of estimation and measurement.

Activity Board

- Ask the children to collect a variety of materials, such as string and pieces of wool, that will fit into a small box. Make a list of the items and their estimated lengths. Ask the children to measure the items and record the estimation, measurement and difference.

Spooky Measures

Display

- Create Spooky Castle Windows to display the children's work on using small measures. Ask the children to make bats, moons, stars and spiders to add to the display.

Oral and Mental Activities

- Use an OHT to show the children a section of a ruler. Concentrate on identifying centimetres.

- Ask the children to estimate 1cm using their thumb and finger.

- With the children working in pairs' ask each child to draw 1cm on paper, then swap papers to check their estimate.

- Ask the children to look closely at the measures which come between the centimetre lines (millimetres).

- Provide children with a hand lens and a variety of very small objects, some measuring only a few centimetres and some less than a centimetre, for example a bead, a width of an elastic band, a pin and an earring. Ask the children to measure their objects with the help of the hand lens. Write down the measurements of length and width on paper, then label and place their object alongside.

- In groups, the children can order their objects, with the appropriate measures displayed.

Practical and Recorded Activities

- Provide the children with a selection of small paper cut-outs of bats, moons and stars. An easy and effective alternative is to give the children sticky dots or stars.

- Invite the children to stick them at random on a sheet of paper. Ask them to join the stars, moons and bats using a gold pen.

- Ask the children to estimate the distance between the bats, moons and stars, then measure accurately in centimetres and millimetres. Note the difference between their estimation and measurement. Use a hand lens to help check the accuracy of their work. Mount and display the work in the shape of castle windows.

Activity Board

- Invite the children to fill a matchbox with small objects, some measuring more or less than a centimetre. Ask them to write a list of contents and their estimated measurements to fit in the matchbox. Use the objects and estimates as a basis for measurement in class, checking the work with the aid of a hand lens.

- Make a little measuring book (see page 27) to record and display their work and the vocabulary used. The children should record their estimate, measurement and difference for each object.

Perfumery

Display

- Create a Perfumery display as a starting point and context for work on capacity. Add a variety of perfume bottles, labelled and calibrated by the children.

Oral and Mental Activities

- Use an OHT with acetates showing containers with calibrated measures or use actual calibrated measures containing coloured water to support the children in their reading of different calibrations.

- Show the children a jug of coloured liquid and ask them on the command 'Show Me' to decide if the jug contains more or less than a given amount of liquid. Is there more or less than half a litre of liquid? Or ask the children to decide on a specific amount of liquid, for example: Does the jug contain approximately 100ml?

- Ask the children what the measure would read if 10, 20, 30 or 40ml of liquid were added. Ask how much more liquid would be needed to make a litre.

- Pose problems, for example:

  - John has 550ml of orange juice, how much more would he need to make a litre?

  - Which is the largest amount of liquid: half a litre or 650ml? Ask the children to write down the answer and 'Show Me'.

  - Ask questions to see if the children understand which measures are appropriate to use, for example to measure bathwater, medicine or a glass of orange juice.

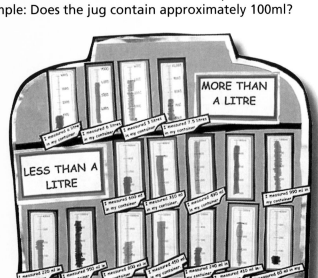

Practical and Recorded Activities

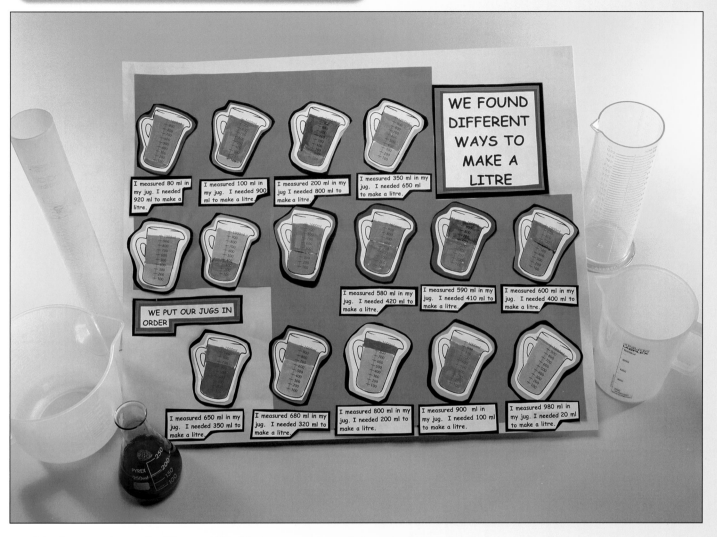

I measured 80 ml in my jug. I needed 920 ml to make a litre.

I measured 100 ml in my jug. I needed 900 ml to make a litre.

I measured 200 ml in my jug I needed 800 ml to make a litre.

I measured 350 ml in my jug. I needed 650 ml to make a litre.

WE FOUND DIFFERENT WAYS TO MAKE A LITRE

WE PUT OUR JUGS IN ORDER

I measured 580 ml in my jug. I needed 420 ml to make a litre.

I measured 590 ml in my jug. I needed 410 ml to make a litre.

I measured 600 ml in my jug. I needed 400 ml to make a litre

I measured 650 ml in my jug. I needed 350 ml to make a litre.

I measured 680 ml in my jug. I needed 320 ml to make a litre.

I measured 800 ml in my jug. I needed 200 ml to make a litre.

I measured 900 ml in my jug. I needed 100 ml to make a litre.

I measured 980 ml in my jug. I needed 20 ml to make a litre.

- Display a variety of calibrated liquid measures containing varying amounts of coloured water. Invite the children to read the calibrations. Record on blank calibrated measuring sheets.

- Order the measures according to the amount of coloured water in each container.

- Provide the children with a variety of interesting containers. Ask them to estimate how much liquid each container will hold. Provide them with the opportunity to fill the container and measure the contents using a calibrated measure.

- Ask the children to draw their container and record the liquid it will hold. Ask them to generate questions about their containers and record them.

- Choose the most interesting containers to draw, label and present as part of the Perfumery display.

- Working in groups, pour a random amount of coloured water into a calibrated litre measure. Measure the amount of the water, estimate the amount of additional water required to make a litre and then pour it into the container. Record the work in two colours on printed litre jugs.

Activity Board

- Display several interesting potion bottles labelled with the different amounts of liquid they can hold. Invite the children to prepare a potion to make their friend invisible. For example: Which combinations of bottles could you use to make 2 litres of your potion?

What Time Is It?

Display

- Create an interactive Time display to illustrate time differences. Display pairs of watches showing time differences. Attach the hands by using mapping pins so that times and questions can be changed. Arrange questions and answers around the watches.

Oral and Mental Activities

- Using a counting stick, ask the children to count on in tens until they reach 60. Ask which numbers are half of 60, a quarter of 60 and a third of 60.

- Use intersecting card circles or paper-plate clocks for 'Show Me' activities. Show the passage of a quarter of an hour, half an hour and 45 minutes.

- Ask the children simple time difference problems. For example: Swimming lasts for 15 minutes. It starts at 3.35 pm. What time does it finish? Use small teaching clocks to 'Show Me' the time it finishes.

- Use the display watches to show the start and finish times of swimming. It is important that the children have the opportunity to see the passage of time.

- Estimate the time on a clock on which the minute hand is missing. For example:
  - What time might swimming have started?
  - What time might swimming have ended if you swam for 25 minutes and took 15 minutes to get dressed?

Practical and Recorded Activities

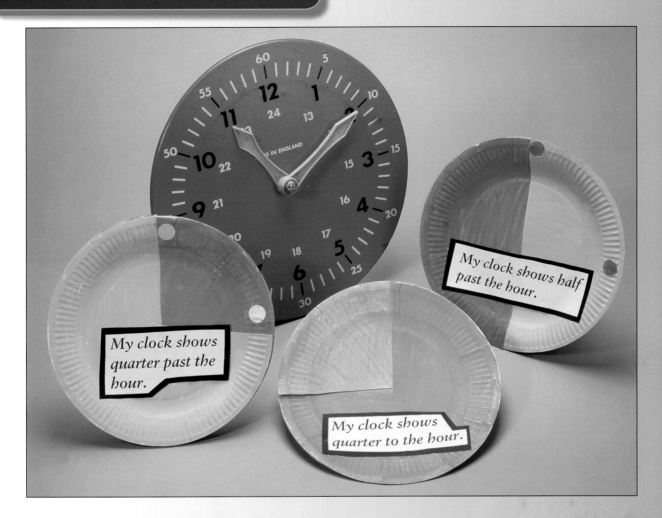

- Invite the children to make their own clocks using two intersecting paper plates or card circles. Paint each plate a different colour and use it to show the passage of time.

- Make card watches, attaching the hands with mapping pins to allow changes in time. Devise time difference questions, for example: Face painting starts at 2.55pm and lasts 25 minutes. What time will it finish? Show both times using the two watches.

- Provide clocks with only the minute hand showing. The children have to use their problem-solving skills to answer simple questions such as: Grandma put the jam tarts in the oven at half past the hour. She left them for 20 minutes to bake, but they were not ready and needed five more minutes. What time could she have put in the jam tarts and what time would she have taken them out?

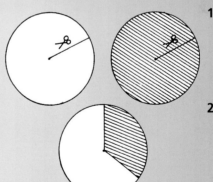

1. Cut each paper plate down the radius.

2. Intersect the two plates so that one moves over the top of the other.

Activity Board

- Set puzzles about Puffing Billy, a miniature railway train that takes passengers along the coast at the seaside. The journey takes 25 minutes to get to Castle Rock, 10 minutes to load passengers and 30 minutes to get back to the station. What time will Puffing Billy arrive at Castle Rock and back to the station if it starts at ... (show the time on a card clock face).

- Change the starting times, the time taken and the number of journeys each day.

Calendar Calculations

- Use clip art to create 12 birthday images, for example a cake, a present, a balloon and an invitation. Use these to create a label for each month of the year.

- Use photographs or digital pictures of each child in the class to be placed on a large birthday chart. Add banners, parcels, birthday cakes or cards to the display.

Oral and Mental Activities

- Provide a variety of calendars. Use the current month to generate mathematical questions. For example: How many Saturdays are there in the month?

- Ask the children how many months there are in a year. Name the months, write them down and record how many days there are in each month.

- Ask the children to write down the month of their birthday. Invite the children to move around the room whispering the month in which they were born and to join up with other children born in that month.

- Collate a tally chart showing the spread of children and months in which they were born.

- Ask the children to write down the date of their birthday and to order the dates within their month group.

- Working in groups sharing the same month, ask the children to add their birthdays to a calendar. Ask:
  - Which month has the most/least birthdays?
  - What is the difference between the most/least number of birthdays in a month?
  - Which month has no birthdays?
  - Are more children born in a particular month or on a particular day?

Practical and Recorded Activities

- Invite the children to place their photograph on the class birthday chart.

- Give each child the responsibility of sending a birthday card to the child whose birthday follows theirs. (Children are not expected to buy cards, but a pool of cards can be made using clip art, or old cards can be collected and recycled.) The birthday chart works well when every child in the school is included.

- Design and make envelopes to fit the cards.

- Create a computer database of birthdays for the whole class or school and display each child's birthday.

- Use the current month on the calendar to investigate mathematical patterns (see diagram). For example, ask the children:

  - to find out what happens to the numbers as they go across and down the calendar. (They go across in ones and down in sevens.)
  - to find three numbers in a row that have totals of 7 (1, 2, 4), 32 (9, 10, 13), 75 (24, 25, 26).
  - to find three numbers which are next to one another in a vertical line and have a sum of 45 (8, 15, 22).
  - to find three numbers which are next to one another in a diagonal line and have a sum of 51 (11, 17, 23).

Calendar						
①	②	3	④	5	6	7
8	⑨	⑩	11	12	⑬	14
15	16	17	18	19	20	21
22	23	㉔	㉕	㉖	27	28
29	30	31				

Activity Board

- Display calendars for different months of the year. Challenge the children to find:
  - four numbers which form a square that have a sum of 20 (1, 2, 8, 9).
  - four numbers which form a square and have a sum of 60 (11, 12, 18, 19).

- Will these numbers appear in a square every month on the same day?

One Potato, Two Potatoes

Display

- Create a Potato display to support work on weight/mass. Make and display three card scales with movable dials, add kilogram weights and present the children's weighing results on potatoes arranged around the display.

Oral and Mental Activities

- Collect a variety of different-shaped weights of the same measure.

- Invite named children to hold a kilogram measure in their hand. Ask:
  - What does it feel like?
  - What else do they know that weighs about the same/has a similar mass?

- Repeat the activity for a variety of weights. Ensure that all the children have the opportunity to hold the metric weights in their hand.

- Draw a number line and label it 0–1000 grams in 100-gram intervals. Invite the children to show half, a quarter and three quarters of a kilogram on the number line.

- Use an OHT to show the children a variety of different scale graduations in 10- or 100-gram intervals. Practise reading the graduated scales, counting on and back in 10s and 100s.

- Place potatoes weighing 500 grams, 250 grams and 100 grams on different scales and ask the children to read the scales and record the weight/mass.

- Provide a variety of commercial packages showing different weights/masses. Ask the children to write down the weights as seen on the packets. Order the packages according to their weight/mass.

Practical and Recorded Activities

- Divide the children into four groups. Provide each group with a set of weighing scales and each child in the group with a potato.

- Each child must estimate the weight/mass of their potato, and then weigh and record it. Record the work on clip-art potato sacks or in small weighing books.

- Ask each group to order the potatoes by weight/mass.

- Display weighing scales and potatoes. Add interactive questions for the children to solve. For example, place two potatoes on the scales and write the question: I wanted 5 kilograms of potatoes, how much more do I need to add to make up this weight/mass? Provide examples of different scales for children to use.

- Provide the children with target weights, for example 1 kilogram, and see how close they get to their target using the potatoes they have weighed.

Activity Board

- Provide a variety of different weighing scales. Ask the children to write instructions for another child to follow to use the scales they have chosen. The children can test their partner's instructions. Accurate instructions can be displayed alongside the scales.

Horse Racing

Display

- Create a Horse Racing display as a starting point and context for work on probability. Select clip-art drawings of horses. Number the horses 1–12. Make a probability line and display the following words: no chance, poor chance, even chance, good chance and certain. Make and display a racetrack with rosette markers representing the horses in the display.

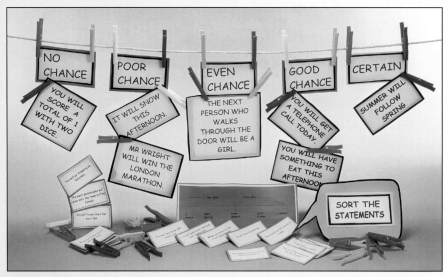

Oral and Mental Activities

- Set up a probability washing line displaying the words: no chance, poor chance, even chance, good chance and certain. Provide a series of statements and ask the children to decide where each statement will go. Peg these to the appropriate label on the line. Ask the children to generate their own statements and attach them to the probability line.

Practical and Recorded Activities

- Make a 'Horse Racing' game. Ask the children to test the game to be sure it is fair. The game consists of children throwing two dice, calculating their total and then moving the horse numbered with that total one square along the racetrack. The first horse to the finishing post is the winner.

- Play the game and keep a tally of the numbers that were thrown using a tally sheet. Ask the following questions:
  - Which horse did not move at all? Why?
  - Which horses had the most moves? Why?
  - Which horse do you think will win? Why?

- Investigate which numbers are most likely to come up by finding all the different ways to make the numbers 1–12 using two dice. Record and display. Find out:
  - Which numbers are the least popular? Why?
  - Which number should be withdrawn from the board? Why?

- Invite the children to play the game and test out their generalisations.

Activity Board

- Draw a probability line on the Activity Board. Ask the children to indicate on the line what they think the chances are of heads or tails coming up out of 20 throws. Ask them to predict before the investigation and give reasons for their prediction. Provide paper and coins for the children to record their investigation.

Crispy Data

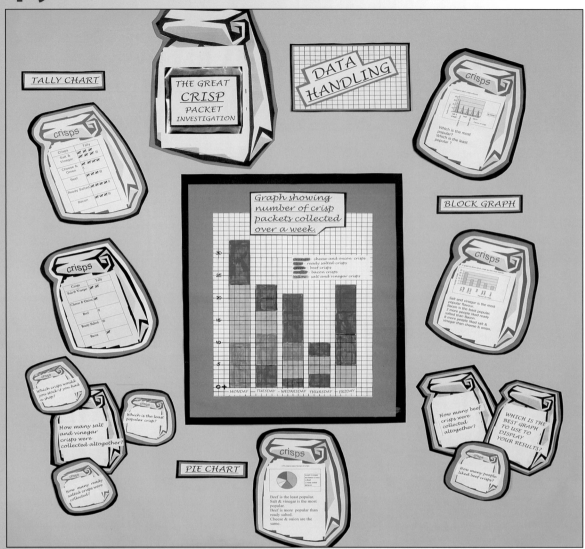

Display

- Use ICT to create a Data-Handling display to present a graphical interpretation of the number and type of crisp packets collected over a week. Use clip art to find images of crisp packets on which to present the children's information. Present the data in a variety of forms, including tally charts, block graphs, line graphs, bar charts and pie charts.

Oral and Mental Activities

- Use the graph showing Favourite Fruit Jellies to practise the skills of interpreting data. Ask the children the following questions:
  - Which is the most popular fruit jelly?
  - Which is the least popular fruit jelly? Explain how you reached your decisions.
  - How many children liked blue fruit jellies best (if each square represents one child)?
  - How many children liked green fruit jellies best?

Graph showing Favourite Fruit Jellies

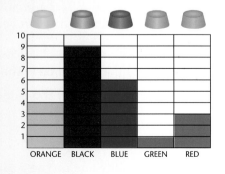

- Change the value of the squares to emphasise the importance of looking to check their values. For example, what if each square represents 2, 5, or 10? Ask the children how they calculate the number of jellies. If they owned a shop, which fruit jellies would they stock/not stock?

Practical and Recorded Activities

- Organise the class into five groups, providing each group with a box containing empty crisp packets collected for one day of the week.

- Ask each group to make a tally chart to show the most popular flavour for each day's findings.

- Invite each group to choose a method of displaying their information (for example, a line chart, a bar chart or pie chart) using the computer. Mount each graph on clip-art crisp packets for display.

- Present the data to other groups and decide which was the best way to display their findings.

- Collate the information from each group and show as a bar chart.

- Ask each group to compose five questions about their data. Mount the questions and add to the crisp-packet display.

- Use IT to display and present information gathered by the children in a subject area of personal interest. Select a question, the answer to which can easily be found by collecting the necessary information.

- Plan the collection of the data, and then process the collected data using a data-handling program for interpretation and discussion.

Activity Board

- If you were to open a shop near to your school, which type of crisp would you stock? Which crisps would you not stock and why? Arrange the crisps in order according to their popularity.

Hands-On (page 8)